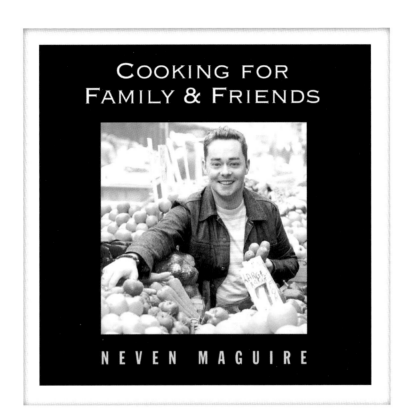

COOKING FOR FAMILY & FRIENDS

NEVEN MAGUIRE

POOLBEG

Published 2004
Poolbeg Press Ltd.
123 Grange Hill, Baldoyle,
Dublin 13, Ireland
Email: poolbeg@poolbeg.com

1 3 5 7 9 10 8 6 4 2

A catalogue record for this book is available from the British Library.

ISBN 1-84223-215-0

Photography by Kieran Harnett
Designed by Steven Hope
Typeset by Patricia Hope in Trebuchet 9/11
Edited by Orla Broderick

Printed by CPI Bath

www.poolbeg.com

Biography

Neven Maguire has been cooking alongside his mother since he was twelve in their award-winning restaurant in Blacklion, Co. Cavan. Although Neven is still in his twenties he has sixteen years of cooking experience behind him and a string of awards to his credit. In 1999 and 2000 he was 'Bushmills' Chef of the Year'. In 2001, Neven represented Ireland in the prestigious 'Bocuse d'Or World Cuisine Competition' in France. His most recent achievements have been 'Jameson Chef of the Year' in 2004 and 'Best Restaurant in Ulster' – Food & Wine Magazine Awards, in both 2003 and 2004. Neven was a well-kept secret known only to foodies until four years ago when he took up residency in the *Open House* studio as chef. Now his name is a byword for elegant, classic cooking.

Acknowledgements

I come from a large family of nine children. Growing up in our house there was never a dull moment, and to this day it is bursting with laughter and love when we congregate. Three years ago when I started to write my first book, I was full of worries and apprehension of the task ahead. Throughout that tentative journey into publishing, I was never alone. My family surrounded me, supported me and encouraged me every step of the way. I share the success of that first book with them.

I also come from a small rural border village called Blacklion in Co. Cavan and I thank God for that good fortune every day. There is an ancient African proverb that says 'It takes a village to raise child'. I couldn't agree more. I am lucky to live amongst a community that cherishes everybody, looks out for each other and takes pride in all their achievements. Like my family, my community has motivated and inspired me in my chosen career.

Some people think that being from a small village can't be good for business. Why don't I move to Dublin? I believe that it is because I'm from Blacklion that I am the chef I am. The surrounding landscape energises me. I cook with herbs, vegetables, meat and poultry that come from this land and that has been reared and grown by people in my community for generations. That's hugely important to me and absolutely vital to my cooking.

Therefore I would like to acknowledge all those who visit our remote bistro and in doing so experience a small part of this life through the food. Equally I would like to express my deep gratitude to colleagues in the food industry who have taken the 'road less travelled' – Paulo Tulio, Ernie Whalley, Georgina Campbell and Sally and John McKenna, to name a few. In visiting us you help sustain many small local businesses and hopefully leave with a greater sense of this magical place.

Finally I would like to thank Kieran Harnett, Orla Broderick and Tyrone Productions for their continued support.

I would like to dedicate this book to Amelda
for all her support and encouragement.

Introduction

This book is for every busy parent, enthusiastic amateur chef or after-work and weekend entertainer. I have divided the recipes into chapters which I think reflect the way we live today. From the most casual last-minute suppers to formal dinner parties and festive celebrations, *Cooking for Family and Friends* presents a selection of balanced and enticing dishes that are all easily achieved.

Mealtimes in our home never follow a pattern. Sometimes I find myself alone with a bacon sandwich after a long night's service in the restaurant. Other times the house is packed with all the family expecting to be fed. From one day to the next, mealtimes vary, not only in the time that they are eaten but who's eating and how long you've got to prepare.

Food has never been more exciting than it is today. With produce from all over the world available in our local shops and supermarkets, it's these inspiring ingredients that I have combined with store-cupboard essentials, an approach that fits in with a busy modern lifestyle.

For me, this book is about showing you how to prepare delicious, hearty and wholesome home-cooked dishes that not only impress but will provide a satisfying and tasty meal. Hope you enjoy them as much as I enjoyed writing about them.

Contents

Smoothies

Serves 4

Smoothies are a family favourite in my house, especially with my sisters. They really are a great way to start the day but are amazingly low in fat!

Peach and Strawberry Smoothie

Ingredients
14oz / 400g can peach slices in natural juice
4oz / 100g fresh or frozen strawberries, plus extra to decorate

$^1/_2$ pint / 300 ml apple juice, well chilled
$^1/_4$ pint / 150ml vanilla yoghurt, well chilled
handful ice cubes

Method Tip the whole can of peaches and juice into a food processor or liquidiser and add the strawberries, apple juice and yoghurt with four of the ice cubes. Blend until smooth.

To Serve Pour the smoothie into tall glasses filled with the rest of the ice cubes. Decorate each glass with a whole strawberry.

Tip Frozen berries are brilliant to use straight from the freezer for smoothies as they instantly cool the mixture down.

Banana, Passion Fruit and Pineapple Smoothie

Serves 4

Use the vanilla yoghurt and skimmed milk straight from the fridge to help keep the smoothies as cold as possible.

Ingredients
2 passion fruit
2 ripe bananas
14oz / 400g can pineapple cubes in natural juice
$^1/_4$ pint / 150ml vanilla yoghurt, well chilled

$^1/_4$ pint / 150ml skimmed milk, well chilled
handful ice cubes
fresh mint sprigs, to decorate

Method Cut the passion fruit in half and scoop the pulp with a teaspoon into a food processor or liquidiser. Peel the bananas and chop the flesh and add to the processor with the whole can of pineapple cubes and juice, yoghurt, milk and four of the ice cubes. Blend until smooth.

To Serve Pour the smoothie into tall glasses filled with the rest of the ice cubes. Decorate each glass with a mint sprig.

Tip Choose dark dimpled passion fruit, which indicates ripeness, and the largest specimens you can find.

Blacklion Porridge with Irish Mist, Honey and Cream

Serves 4

Believe it or not, this outrageously scrumptious concoction is one of our most popular breakfast choices in the restaurant. It's got everything you need to kick-start the day but obviously you can adjust the recipe to your own preference.

Ingredients
3oz / 75g porridge oats (organic if possible)
3/4 pint / 450ml milk
4 dessertspoons clear honey
4 dessertspoons Irish Mist
1/4 pint / 150ml cream (optional)

Method Place the porridge oats in a heavy-based pan with the milk and bring to a simmer, then continue to cook for 8-10 minutes, stirring continuously until the mixture is slightly thickened and smooth.

To Serve Spoon the porridge into warmed serving bowls. Drizzle the honey and Irish Mist over it and finish by pouring over the cream, if liked.

● Tip This takes no more than 10 minutes to prepare so don't be tempted to rush the cooking process as it is important the porridge has a nice dropping consistency.

Poached Apricots with Vanilla, Cinnamon and Greek Yoghurt

Serves 4

This will keep for up to three weeks in the fridge in a rigid plastic container, so it's worth making up a double batch once you are going to the trouble.

Ingredients
2oz / 50g caster sugar
$1/2$ vanilla pod, split
1 cinnamon stick
2 whole star anise
12oz / 350g ready-to-eat dried apricots
$1/4$ pint / 150ml thick Greek yoghurt
fresh mint sprigs, to garnish

Method Place the sugar in a pan with $1/2$ pint / 300ml of water. Add the split vanilla pod, cinnamon stick and star anise. Bring to the boil, then tip in the apricots, reduce the heat and simmer gently for 15 minutes. Remove from the heat and leave to cool.

To Serve Spoon the poached apricots into serving bowls and add a good dollop of Greek yoghurt and garnish with the mint leaves.

Tip Star anise is a pretty star-shaped pod with a flavour that is almost overwhelmingly anise liquoricy, but with deeper spicy undertones.

Eggs Benedict with Bacon and Mushrooms

Serves 4

Everyone loves Eggs Benedict for breakfast and once you've mastered how to poach the eggs, the rest is a doddle. I normally make mine in advance so that I just have to reheat them as needed.

Ingredients
4 large eggs (preferably free-range or organic)
2 tablespoons white wine vinegar
4 large flat cap mushrooms, trimmed
2oz / 50g butter
4 rindless streaky bacon rashers
9oz / 250g baby spinach leaves
2 bread baps, split in half

For the Butter Sauce
3$\frac{1}{2}$ fl oz/ 100ml cream
4oz / 100g butter, diced and well chilled
1 teaspoon Dijon mustard
1 teaspoon fresh lemon juice
1 tablespoon snipped fresh chives, plus extra whole chives to garnish
1 tablespoon chopped fresh tarragon
salt and freshly ground black pepper

Method To poach the eggs, heat 4 pints / 2.25 litres of water in a large pan. Add the vinegar and bring to the boil. When the water is bubbling, break the eggs in one by one, then reduce the heat to very low (or move the pan to the edge of the heat) and leave to simmer for 3 minutes. Remove each egg with a slotted spoon and plunge into a bowl of iced water. When cold, trim any ragged edges from the cooked white, then return to the water and chill until needed.

Preheat the grill to high. Smear the mushrooms all over with half of the butter and season generously. Arrange on the grill rack gill-side down and cook for 4-5 minutes, then turn over and add the bacon. Cook the bacon and mushrooms for another 4-5 minutes until tender, turning the bacon once until crisp and lightly golden. Drain the bacon on kitchen paper and keep the mushrooms warm.

Meanwhile, heat a small pan. Add the remaining butter and once it has melted, tip in the spinach. Season to taste and stir occasionally for a minute or so until the leaves are tender and bright green. Drain off the excess water and keep warm.

To make the butter sauce, bring the cream to the boil in a pan. Whisk in the butter, remove from the heat and then whisk in the mustard, lemon juice, chives and tarragon. Season to taste.

To Serve Add the poached eggs to a pan of boiling salted water and just heat through for 1-2 minutes. Remove with a slotted spoon and drain on kitchen paper. Meanwhile, toast the split baps on the grill rack and arrange half on each warmed serving plate. Place a grilled flat cap mushroom on top and spoon over the wilted spinach. Top with a poached egg and arrange bacon to one side, then pour over some of the butter sauce and garnish with the whole chives.

Tip For a vegetarian option, omit the bacon and serve with grilled tomatoes on the side.

Smoked Salmon, Rocket and Cream Cheese Bagel

Serves 4

This is classic New York deli bagel where smoked salmon is known as lox. I must admit this took a bit of getting used to when I first spent time over there.

Ingredients
4 bagels, split in half
4oz / 100g full-fat cream cheese or ricotta
finely grated rind and juice of $1/2$ lemon
1 teaspoon snipped fresh chives
1 tablespoon finely diced red onion
2oz / 50g wild rocket
8 large smoked salmon slices
lemon wedges, to garnish

Method Preheat the grill to high and arrange the split bagels cut-side up on a grill rack. Toast until crisp and golden. Meanwhile, place the cream cheese or ricotta in a bowl with the lemon rind and juice, chives and red onion. Season and mix until well combined.

To Serve Spread the cream cheese mixture on top of each toasted bagel. Next arrange the rocket on top with the smoked salmon slices. Place on serving plates and garnish with the lemon wedges.

Tip Bagels are perfect for freezing and I always keep some tucked away for those unplanned mornings after the night before...

Egg and Parma Ham Croissant with Tomato Relish

Serves 4

These filled croissants are always a winner at breakfast and are an excellent way of using up day-old croissants.

Ingredients
8 slices Parma ham
4 large croissants
2 tablespoons olive oil
4 eggs

For the Tomato Relish
1 tablespoon olive oil

2 ripe vine tomatoes, finely chopped
2 spring onions, finely chopped
1 tablespoon balsamic vinegar
large pinch caster sugar
2 fresh basil leaves, chopped
salt and freshly ground black pepper
vine roasted tomatoes, to serve (optional – page 31)
fresh parsley sprigs, to garnish

Method To make the tomato relish, heat the olive oil in a pan. Add the tomatoes, spring onions, balsamic vinegar, sugar and basil leaves and simmer gently for 10-15 minutes until the tomatoes have softened and the relish is slightly reduced. Remove from the heat, season to taste and set aside until needed.

Meanwhile, preheat the grill and heat a large non-stick frying pan. Arrange the Parma ham slices on a grill rack and cook for 2 minutes, without turning, until crisp. Slice open the croissants and lightly toast, then spread over the tomato relish. Arrange two slices of the crispy Parma ham on each of the bottom halves in an overlapping layer.

Add the oil to the heated frying pan and swirl to coat the base evenly. Break in the eggs and cook for 2 minutes, or longer if you prefer the egg less runny, basting the oil over the yolks to ensure even cooking.

To Serve Using a fish slice, carefully lift the eggs on to the Parma ham and season with pepper, then place the top of a croissant on each one. Arrange on warmed serving plates with the vine roasted tomatoes, if liked, and garnish with the parsley sprigs.

●**Tip** Use crispy streaky bacon rashers or hand-carved cooked ham as an alternative to the Parma ham.

Egg and Bacon Breakfast Roll

Serves 4

This ultimate breakfast on the go is something that you can really get your teeth into and is perfect for soaking up any excess alcohol after a night on the tiles...

Ingredients
4 eggs
8 rindless streaky bacon rashers
1 ciabatta loaf
6 tablespoons tomato relish (shop-bought or home-made page 11)

6oz / 175g Gruyère or Cheddar, grated
salt and freshly ground black pepper
fresh parsley sprigs, to garnish

Method Preheat the grill. Place the eggs in a small pan and just cover with boiling water, then cook for 8-10 minutes until hard-boiled. Drain and rinse under cold running water, then remove the shells and cut each egg into slices.

Meanwhile, arrange the bacon on a grill rack and cook for about 5 minutes, turning once until crisp and golden, then cut into pieces.

Split the ciabatta in half and toast under the grill, then spread the tomato relish over. Scatter the hard-boiled egg slices and bacon pieces over, then season to taste. Sprinkle the Gruyère or Cheddar on top and arrange on the grill rack. Cook for 3-4 minutes until bubbling and golden.

To Serve Slice the ciabatta into pieces on the diagonal and arrange on warmed serving plates. Garnish with the parsley sprigs.

Tip Try replacing the crispy streaky bacon with chopped cooked sausages and use the best quality you can afford.

Beef and Button-Mushroom Casserole

Serves 6-8

Casseroles are simply the easiest meals to prepare. First you do all your peeling, slicing and sautéing, then you pop everything into a large pot with a lid and leave it in the oven for a couple of hours. In the meantime you can go for a walk, watch a movie, or mow the lawn and later on you can settle down to a hearty, warming feast. Perfect on a cold crisp day when all the family is looking for something piping hot.

Ingredients
2 tablespoons olive oil
1oz / 25 g butter
2 lb / 900 g topside or stewing beef, trimmed and cut into 1in / 2.5cm cubes
1 pint / 600ml red wine
1 tablespoon tomato puree
1¹/₂ pints / 900ml beef or chicken stock (from stock cubes is fine)
1 bay leaf
1 teaspoon chopped fresh thyme
1 tablespoon Worcestershire sauce
1 lb / 450 g button mushrooms, halved

8oz / 225 g shallots, trimmed and peeled (with root intact)

For the Parsley Dumplings
4oz / 100g self-raising flour, plus extra for dusting
4oz / 100g fresh white breadcrumbs
1 tablespoon wholegrain mustard
5oz / 150g butter
2 teaspoons chopped fresh thyme
2 tablespoons chopped fresh parsley, plus extra to garnish
2 eggs, lightly beaten
salt and freshly ground black pepper
boiled floury potatoes, to serve

Method Preheat the oven to 200C/400F/Gas 6. Heat half of the oil and butter in a heavy-based casserole with a lid over a high heat. When the butter is foaming, tip in about a quarter of the beef and cook for 3-4 minutes, stirring regularly with a wooden spoon to seal in the flavour. Transfer to a bowl with a slotted spoon and set aside. Repeat in batches until all of the meat has been browned, adding extra olive oil and butter as necessary.

Pour a quarter of the wine into the casserole and de-glaze with a wooden spoon by scraping the caramelised meat residue from the base. Stir in the tomato puree and mix thoroughly to combine. Return the beef to the casserole with the rest of the wine, the stock, bay leaf, thyme, Worcestershire sauce and season to taste. Bring to the boil, then cover and place in the middle of the oven for 1 hour 45 minutes, stirring every half an hour or so.

Reduce the oven temperature to 180C/350F/Gas 4. Take the casserole out of the oven and stir in the mushrooms and shallots, then return to the oven without the lid for 25 minutes while you prepare the parsley dumplings. Place the flour, breadcrumbs, mustard and butter into a food processor or liquidiser and whiz to a crumb consistency. Add the thyme, parsley, eggs and season to taste. Blitz again briefly until the mixture forms a fairly moist dough. Using floured hands, roll the dough into six to eight large even-sized balls. Add the dumplings to the casserole and cook for another 20 minutes or until the dumplings have cooked through and puffed up.

To Serve Ladle the stew into warmed wide-rimmed serving bowls and garnish with parsley. Place the boiled floury potatoes on the side to soak up the rich juices.

●**Tip** This stew would taste even better the following day and is a great crowd-pleaser – simply double or treble the quantity. Make sure you've got a big enough casserole pot first!

Shepherd's Pie Jackets

Serves 4-8

This variation on classic shepherd's pie can also be made with the leftovers of the Sunday joint. It's the perfect way to get children to eat vegetables without even realising it.

Ingredients
4 large baking potatoes
1 tablespoon olive oil
1lb / 450g lean minced beef
1 onion, chopped
2 carrots, diced
1lb / 450g button mushrooms, sliced
1 garlic clove, crushed
2 tablespoons Worcestershire sauce

1/2 pint / 300ml beef stock (from a cube is fine)
1 tablespoon tomato puree
1 teaspoon chopped fresh thyme
1 tablespoon chopped fresh parsley
1 tablespoon milk
2oz / 50g butter
4oz / 100g Cheddar, grated (Dubliner, if possible)
salt and freshly ground black pepper
steamed broccoli, sugar snap peas and courgettes, to serve

Method Preheat the oven at 180C/350F/Gas 4. Pierce the potatoes a couple of times to prevent them from splitting, then rub them with a little salt to help give them an extra-crispy skin, and place directly on the oven shelf. Bake for about 1 hour or until slightly softened when squeezed. Remove from the oven and leave until cool enough to handle.

Meanwhile, heat the oil in a large sauté pan with a lid, then tip in the minced beef, onion, carrots, mushrooms and garlic. Sauté for 10 minutes until the onion is golden and the mince is lightly browned, breaking up any lumps of mince with the back of a wooden spoon. Stir in the Worcestershire sauce and cook for another 2 minutes. Pour in the stock and then add the tomato puree and thyme, stirring until well combined. Cover and simmer for 20 minutes or until the mince is cooked through and completely tender. Finally stir in the parsley and season to taste.

Preheat the grill. Cut each cooked potato in half lengthways, scoop out the flesh into a bowl leaving a thin layer, then quickly mash with the milk and butter. Season to taste and beat with a wooden spoon until smooth. Place the scooped-out potato skins in a shallow roasting tin and spoon in the cooked mince mixture. Spoon the mashed potato into a piping bag with a 1in / 2.5cm nozzle and pipe on top of the filled potato skins. Sprinkle with the Cheddar and place under the grill until cheese is bubbling and golden and the potatoes are completely heated through.

To Serve Arrange the shepherd's pie jackets on warmed serving plates with some steamed broccoli, sugar snap peas and courgettes.

Tip If you're short of time give the baked potatoes a head start in the microwave on high for 5 minutes, and halve the cooking time.

Chilli Con Carne with Spicy Wedges

Serves 6-8

There are so many different versions of chilli but I have to admit this version is pretty damn good! Perfect for feeding the family and a wonderful freezer standby for nights when you just can't face cooking.

Ingredients

4 tablespoons olive oil
2lb / 900g rump or braising steak, trimmed and cut into 1in / 2.5 cm strips
2 onions, chopped
1 teaspoon hot chilli powder
1 tablespoon ground paprika
1 teaspoon ground cumin
1 teaspoon ground coriander
2 tablespoons dark muscovado sugar

1 pint /600ml beef stock (from a cube is fine)
3 garlic cloves, crushed
1 tablespoon tomato puree
2lb / 900g ripe tomatoes, roughly chopped
1½ lb / 675g potatoes
1 tablespoon Cajun seasoning
2 x 14oz / 400g cans red kidney beans, drained and rinsed
salt and freshly ground black pepper
crème fraîche and fresh coriander leaves, to garnish

Method Heat half the olive oil in a large heavy-based pan until very hot. Sauté half the beef strips for 10 minutes until well browned. Drain with a slotted spoon and set aside. Repeat with the remaining beef.

Add the onions to the pan with the chilli powder, paprika, cumin, coriander and sugar. Fry very gently for 8 minutes until the onions are golden and well caramelised, stirring occasionally. Tip in the browned beef strips with the stock, garlic, tomato puree and tomatoes. Bring to the boil, then reduce the heat and simmer for 1 hour, stirring occasionally.

Meanwhile, preheat the oven to 200C/400F/Gas 6. Cut the potatoes into even-sized wedges. Place in a pan of boiling salted water and blanch for 2-3 minutes, then quickly drain. Put the remaining olive oil in a large roasting tin with a teaspoon of salt and the Cajun seasoning. Add the wedges and toss until they are all well coated in the flavoured oil, then arrange them in rows 'sitting' upright on their skins. Bake for 35-40 minutes until tender and lightly golden, with an extra 10-15 minutes if you like them really crunchy.

Add the kidney beans to the beef mixture and simmer for another 20 minutes until the beef is meltingly tender. Season to taste.

To Serve Spoon the chilli con carne into warmed wide-rimmed serving bowls set on plates and arrange the spicy potato wedges around the edge. Garnish with a dollop of crème fraîche and a sprinkling of the coriander leaves.

⬤ Tip This chilli is also delicious served with tortilla chips, baked potatoes, warm pitta bread or Mexican spiced rice instead of the spicy potato wedges.

Pork Sausages with Onion Marmalade, Leek and Parsnip Mash

Serves 6

We all adore sausage and mash – it has to be one of my favourite comfort foods. Experiment with the type of pork sausage you use – most good butchers and supermarkets now have a wide range of premium lines available, such as Toulouse or Pork and leek.

Ingredients
12 pork sausages (good quality)
2 tablespoons redcurrant jelly
1 teaspoon fresh lemon juice
2 tablespoons olive oil
14oz / 400g red onions, chopped
2 tablespoons red wine vinegar
2 tablespoons light muscovado sugar
1 tablespoon dark soy sauce

For the Leek and Parsnip Mash
1$1/2$ lb / 675g leeks, sliced
1$1/2$ lb / 675g parsnips, quartered
1 garlic clove, peeled
3$1/2$ fl oz / 100ml milk
1 tablespoon chopped fresh parsley
1 tablespoon freshly grated Parmesan
salt and freshly ground black pepper
fresh chervil sprigs, to garnish (optional)

Method Preheat the oven to 200C/400F/Gas 6. Place the sausages in a small roasting tin. Mix together the redcurrant jelly and lemon juice in a small bowl and spoon it over the sausages, then roast for 35 minutes, turning them once halfway through the cooking time.

Meanwhile, make the mash. Place the leeks, parsnips and garlic in a pan of salted water. Bring to the boil, then reduce the heat and simmer for 15-20 minutes or until the parsnips are completely tender. Drain and return to the pan to allow them to dry out for 5 minutes over a low heat.

Heat the olive oil in a frying pan and gently fry the red onions for 15 minutes, turning regularly until softened but not coloured. Add the vinegar, sugar and soy sauce and cook for another 5 minutes until the onions are really tender. Season to taste.

To finish the mash, heat the milk in a pan until it is warm, then pour into a food processor or liquidiser. Add the leeks, parsnips and garlic mixture with the parsley and Parmesan. Blend until smooth, then return the puree to the pan and reheat over a low heat until completely warmed through.

To Serve Arrange the leek and parsnip mash on warmed serving plates and place the sausages to the side. Add a dollop of the onion marmalade and garnish with chervil sprigs, if liked.

Tip The leek and parsnip mash can be made several hours in advance and simply reheated on high in the microwave for a couple of minutes when you are ready to serve.

Ham and Mozzarella Pizza with Rocket

Serves 6

Pizza is the perfect munching food for an evening in front of the TV with a good bottle of red wine for the adults. What more could you ask for? The tomato sauce will keep for up to 4 days in the fridge, or you could always use one of the good quality shop-bought varieties.

Ingredients
3 shop-bought pizza bases, each about 9in / 22cm
6oz / 175g cooked ham, chopped
4oz / 100g sun-dried tomatoes, chopped
4oz / 100g rocket
2 x 5oz / 150g balls mozzarella, grated
4 tablespoons chopped fresh basil

For the Tomato Sauce
1 tablespoon olive oil
1 small onion, chopped
1 garlic clove, crushed
1lb / 450g ripe vine tomatoes, chopped
3½ fl oz / 100ml dry white wine
2 tablespoons tomato puree
½ pint / 300ml vegetable stock or water

1 tablespoon chopped fresh oregano or basil
salt and freshly ground black pepper
lightly dressed mixed salad, to serve

Method   To make the tomato sauce, heat the olive oil in a pan and sauté the onion, garlic and tomatoes for 5 minutes until softened but not coloured. Pour in the wine and reduce by half, then stir in tomato puree, mixing well to combine. Pour in the stock or water and add the oregano or basil, then simmer for 10 minutes until slightly reduced and thickened, stirring occasionally. Season to taste and set aside until cool.

Preheat the oven to 200C/400F/Gas 6. Spread the cooled tomato sauce evenly over the pizza bases. Sprinkle over the ham and sun-dried tomatoes and then scatter the rocket on top. Cover with the mozzarella and finish with the basil. Bake in batches (or use two ovens) directly on the oven shelf for 15 minutes or until the pizza bases are crisp and the mozzarella is bubbling and lightly golden.

To Serve   Cut each pizza into slices and arrange on warmed serving plates with some of the salad.

VARIATIONS

Italian Parma, Pepperoni and Olive Pizza   Scatter 4oz / 100g each chopped Parma ham and pepperoni, one sliced courgette, one sliced red pepper, 4oz / 100g black pitted olives, 10oz / 300g grated mozzarella and two teaspoons chopped fresh thyme over the tomato-covered pizza bases and cook as described above.

Chicken Tikka Pizza   Cut four skinless chicken breast fillets into chunks and place in a bowl. Add four tablespoons tikka paste and eight tablespoons natural yoghurt. Season to taste, mix well to combine, then cover with clingfilm and chill for 1 hour to allow the flavours to combine. Preheat the grill and arrange the chicken on a foil-lined grill rack, shaking off any excess marinade. Cook for 8-10 minutes, turning occasionally until cooked through and lightly charred. Leave to cool a little and then cut into cubes. Sprinkle over the tomato-covered pizza bases and arrange 10oz / 300g sliced buffalo mozzarella on top, then cook as described above and garnish with fresh coriander leaves.

Mixed Mushroom, Onion and Goat's Cheese Pizza   Heat one tablespoon olive oil in a frying pan and sauté one red onion and two crushed garlic cloves for 5 minutes until softened but not coloured. Season to taste and scatter over the tomato-covered pizza bases. Add 8oz / 225g chopped mixed mushrooms (such as oyster, button and/or chestnut) and 9oz / 250g goat's cheese cubes (good quality such as Corrleggey). Cook as described above and then drizzle over three tablespoons shop-bought or homemade pesto.

Chicken Casserole with Sweet Potatoes

Serves 6-8

When you are in the mood for a real winter warmer that has tonnes of flavour, appeals to all the family and takes very little time to get in the oven compared to traditional casseroles, you can't go far wrong with this recipe.

Ingredients
12 rindless streaky bacon rashers
12 skinless and boneless chicken thighs, trimmed
2 tablespoons plain flour
3 tablespoons olive oil
2 onions, cut into wedges
2 sweet potatoes, peeled and cut into cubes (preferably orange-fleshed)

2 garlic cloves, crushed
10oz / 300g flat mushrooms, sliced
1 bay leaf
2 tablespoons redcurrant jelly
grated rind of 1 orange
9fl oz / 250ml red wine
1 pint / 600ml chicken stock (from a cube is fine)
1 tablespoon chopped fresh parsley

1 tablespoon toasted flaked almonds
salt and freshly ground black pepper
mashed potatoes, to serve

Method Preheat the oven to 200C/400F/Gas 6. Stretch each rasher with the back of a table knife and then use to wrap around a chicken thigh. Season the flour on a flat plate and use to lightly coat the bacon-wrapped chicken thighs. Heat the oil in a large casserole with a lid and cook the wrapped chicken thighs in batches until lightly browned all over. Arrange on a plate and set aside.

Reduce the heat of the casserole, add the onions and sweet potatoes, then sauté for 5 minutes until golden. Add the garlic, then sprinkle in the remaining seasoned flour and cook for 1 minute, stirring to prevent the mixture sticking.

Add the mushrooms, bay leaf, redcurrant jelly and orange rind and then pour in red wine and stock. Bring to the boil, then reduce the heat and return the chicken to the casserole. Cover and cook for 1 hour or until the chicken is completely tender and the sauce has thickened slightly. Season to taste.

To Serve Sprinkle the casserole with the parsley and flaked almonds, then place on the table with a large bowl of mash to mop up all those delicious juices.

●Tip When it comes to chicken I think that thighs have the best flavour and are the most succulent, but by all means use small skinless chicken breast fillets and just cook as described above.

Seafood Paella

Serves 6-8

This Spanish rice dish originates in Valencia, and the name actually refers to the traditional cooking vessel, a paellera. They only cost a couple of euro and are well worth bringing home from your hols.

Ingredients
3½ fl oz / 100ml olive oil
8 chicken thighs
5 oz / 150g smoked bacon lardons
1 onion, chopped
1 red pepper, seeded, cored and sliced
2 garlic cloves, crushed
4 tomatoes, roughly chopped
7oz / 200g long grain rice
1 teaspoon ground paprika

¼ pint / 150ml dry white wine
¾ pint / 450ml chicken stock
1 teaspoon saffron strands
1 teaspoon chopped fresh thyme
1oz / 25g butter
2lb / 900g mussels, cleaned
1lb / 450g packet mixed seafood, (including squid and prawns) thawed if frozen
cooked tiger prawns and chopped fresh parsley, to garnish
crusty bread, to serve

Method Heat half of the oil in a large paella or sauté pan with a lid. Add the chicken thighs and fry for 5 minutes until golden, turning regularly. Add the bacon and sauté for another 5 minutes until the bacon is just cooked through, then remove the chicken and bacon from the pan using a slotted spoon, and drain on kitchen paper. Set aside.

Heat the remaining oil in the pan. Add the onion, red pepper, garlic and tomatoes and sauté for 5 minutes until softened. Stir in the rice and paprika and cook for 1 minute until well coated. Mix half the wine in a jug with the stock and saffron, then pour into the pan. Return chicken and bacon to the pan with the thyme. Bring to the boil, then reduce heat, cover and simmer for 15-20 minutes until the rice and chicken are tender and all the liquid has been absorbed.

Meanwhile, melt the butter in a separate large pan with a lid. Add the mussels and remaining wine. Bring to the boil, then cover and simmer for 3-4 minutes, shaking the pan halfway through. All the mussels should now have opened – discard any that have not. Fold the mixed seafood into the paella pan until heated through. Add the mussels and a little of their cooking juices – just be careful not to make it too soupy.

To Serve Garnish the paella with the cooked tiger prawns and parsley, then place on the table. Serve with a basket of crusty bread.

Tip Most supermarkets and fishmongers now stock packets of mixed seafood that are perfect to use in this dish; otherwise make up your own selection using what's available.

Papperdelle Pasta with Prawns, Saffron and Tomatoes

Serves 4

The best way to treat good seafood is to treat it simply and this recipe is perfect for lazy summer evenings when you just want something light.

Ingredients
2 tablespoons olive oil
1 onion, finely chopped
2 garlic cloves, crushed
1 small fennel bulb, finely chopped
1 celery stick, finely chopped
1 tablespoon chopped fresh thyme
1 teaspoon grated orange rind
1 teaspoon saffron threads
1 tablespoon tomato puree

$1/4$ pint / 150ml dry white wine
$1/4$ pint / 150ml vegetable stock (from a cube is fine)
3 ripe vine tomatoes, seeded and diced
1lb / 450g dried papperdelle pasta
$1^1/_2$ lb / 675g cleaned and peeled Dublin Bay prawns, thawed if frozen
salt and freshly ground black pepper
fresh dill sprigs, to garnish
lightly dressed mixed leaf salad, to serve

Method Heat one tablespoon of the olive oil in a large heavy-based pan. Add the onion, garlic, fennel, celery, thyme and orange rind and cook for 10 minutes, stirring occasionally. Add the saffron and tomato puree and then cook for another 5 minutes until slightly reduced, stirring occasionally.

Pour the wine into the pan and reduce until the liquid has almost completely evaporated. Add the stock and simmer gently for another 15 minutes or until the vegetables are completely tender and the liquid has slightly reduced. Add the tomatoes and allow to just warm through gently. Season to taste.

Meanwhile, heat a frying pan until very hot. Plunge the papperdelle into a large pan of boiling salted water. Stir once and cook for 5 minutes or until *al dente*. Drain quickly and then return to the pan. Tip in the sauce and toss gently until well combined. Add the remaining olive oil to the heated frying pan and sauté the prawns for 2-3 minutes until just cooked through and tender.

To Serve Divide pasta mixture among four warmed pasta bowls and arrange sautéed prawns on top. Garnish with the dill and serve the bowl of salad separately.

●Tip The pasta shape you choose for a dish is entirely up to you but, as a general guide, chunky, gutsy sauces are best with chunky pasta shapes such as fusilli, penne, farfalle or rigatoni, while soft, fluid sauces suit long, slippery pasta, such as linguine, fettuccine, pappardelle or spaghetti.

Chicken and Leek Parcels

Serves 4

I like to use corn or maize-fed chicken breast fillets for this recipe, as they have a much better flavour. The parcels can also be pan-fried in a knob of butter and a couple of tablespoons of olive oil for about 12 minutes or until cooked through and golden brown, turning once.

Ingredients
butter, for greasing
1 small leek, trimmed and finely chopped
4 tablespoons full-fat cream cheese
1 tablespoon finely chopped red onion
1 tablespoon snipped fresh chives
2 tablespoons chopped fresh parsley, plus extra sprigs to garnish
4 x 5oz / 150g skinless chicken breast fillets

6oz / 175g dried white breadcrumbs
2 tablespoons plain flour
2 eggs
2 tablespoons olive oil
4 small vines cherry tomatoes (about 8 on each one)
salt and freshly ground black pepper

Method Preheat the oven to 200C/400F/Gas 6. Lightly grease a baking sheet with the butter. Plunge the leek into a pan of boiling salted water and cook for 2 minutes until just tender, then drain. Tip into a bowl and leave to cool, then mix in the cream cheese, red onion, chives and half of parsley. Mix well.

Using a sharp knife, make a pocket in each chicken breast fillet by cutting horizontally almost all the way through but leaving them attached on one side, then push a quarter of the cream cheese mixture into each one.

Mix the breadcrumbs and remaining parsley on a plate. Place the flour on a separate plate and season generously. Break the eggs into a shallow dish, season and lightly beat. Dust the chicken in the seasoned flour, shaking off any excess. Dip in the beaten egg and then turn in the breadcrumb mixture until evenly coated.

Heat the olive oil in a large frying pan and add the chicken parcels presentation-side down, then cook for 1-2 minutes on each side until lightly golden. Transfer to the buttered greased baking sheet and bake for 10 minutes, then remove from the oven and add the tomato vines. Bake for another 8-10 minutes or until the chicken is cooked through and golden brown and the tomatoes are tender.

To Serve Arrange the chicken and leek parcels on warmed serving plates and carefully place the tomato vines on the side. Garnish with the parsley sprigs.

Tip If time allows, chill the chicken and leek parcels for at least 15 minutes and up to 24 hours to allow the filling and breadcrumb coating to firm up.

Lemon Turkey Stir-Fry

Serves 4

This is really a very simple recipe and one of my favourite ways of serving turkey. It is excellent served with the noodles as it provides a lovely accompanying sauce.

Ingredients

9oz / 250g medium Chinese egg noodles
4 tablespoons lemon marmalade
2 teaspoons cornflour
3 tablespoons fresh lemon juice
1/4 pint / 150ml chicken stock
1 red pepper, cored, seeded and thinly sliced
1 teaspoon freshly grated root ginger

2 tablespoons dark soy sauce
1lb / 450g skinless turkey breast fillet, trimmed and cut into thin strips
6oz / 175g pak choi, cut across into 1in / 2.5cm wide strips
6 spring onions, thinly sliced
salt and freshly ground black pepper

Method Plunge the noodles into a pan of boiling salted water, then remove from the heat and set aside for 4 minutes until tender or according to packet instructions. Drain, cover with clingfilm to keep them warm and set aside.

Place the lemon marmalade in a jug with six tablespoons of boiling water and stir until dissolved. Blend the cornflour in a small bowl with two tablespoons of cold water until smooth. Stir the cornflour paste into the marmalade mixture with the lemon juice and set aside.

Place the stock in a wok or large sauté pan with the red pepper, ginger and soy sauce, then tip in the turkey strips and bring to a simmer. Continue to simmer until the stock has evaporated and the turkey is cooked through, stirring continuously, then continue cooking for another few minutes until the turkey starts to brown.

Add the pak choi to the wok with three tablespoons of water. Toss over a high heat for 2 minutes until just tender but still crunchy. Stir in the spring onions and marmalade mixture and then continue to cook for 2 minutes until the sauce has thickened, stirring. Season to taste.

To Serve Arrange the noodles in warmed serving bowls and then spoon the lemon turkey stir-fry on top.

● Tip If you want to ring in the changes, you could try substituting Chinese cabbage or any other leafy green vegetable for the pak choi.

Bacon Carbonara

Serves 4

Smoked salmon carbonara is also a fantastic supper dish. Simply replace the bacon with strips of smoked salmon, which obviously don't need any cooking, and the parsley with dill.

Ingredients
12oz / 350g spaghetti
1oz / 25g butter
1 onion, finely chopped
1 garlic clove, crushed
8oz / 225g pancetta or rindless streaky bacon rashers, cut into strips

3$^1/_2$ fl oz / 100ml white wine
3 eggs
$^1/_4$ pint / 150ml double cream
2oz / 50g freshly grated Parmesan, plus extra to serve
1 tablespoon chopped fresh parsley
salt and freshly ground black pepper

Method Plunge the spaghetti into a large pan of boiling salted water, stir once and cook for 10-12 minutes or according to packet instructions until *al dente*.

Meanwhile, heat the butter in a large pan. Add the onion and garlic. Cook over a low heat for 5 minutes until softened but not coloured, stirring frequently. Stir in the pancetta or bacon and cook for 6-8 minutes until sizzling and golden, stirring continuously.

Add the white wine to bacon mixture and then reduce to about one tablespoon. Break the eggs into a bowl and add the cream and Parmesan. Season with plenty of freshly ground black pepper and whisk lightly to combine.

Drain the spaghetti and tip it into the pan with the pancetta mixture. Mix well, then quickly pour in the egg mixture and add the parsley. Toss well to combine, then return the pan to the heat and cook gently for 1 minute until the sauce thickens slightly. Season to taste.

To Serve Divide among warmed pasta bowls and sprinkle with black pepper. Place a bowl of freshly grated Parmesan on the table so that people can help themselves.

Tip When returning the sauce to the heat be careful not to overcook, or the eggs will scramble!!

Pea and Pepper Tortilla

Serves 4

This tortilla is a great inexpensive supper or, because it is also excellent served cold, it makes fantastic picnic food cut into wedges and wrapped in clingfilm. In Spain, where it originates you'll often find it in bars served as tapas, cut into small cubes and speared on to cocktail sticks or between two chunks of crusty bread for a portable feast.

Ingredients
8oz / 225g potatoes, cubed
6 eggs
2 tablespoons chopped fresh parsley
1 tablespoon olive oil
1 red pepper, cored, seeded and cut into small chunks

6oz / 175g peas, thawed if frozen
2oz / 50g baby spinach leaves
salt and freshly ground black pepper
fresh coriander sprigs and lemon wedges, to garnish (optional)
lightly dressed green salad, to serve

Method Preheat the grill. Place the potatoes in a pan of boiling salted water and cook for 8 minutes until almost but not quite tender. Drain and dry well on kitchen paper. Break the eggs into a bowl, add the parsley and season to taste, then lightly whisk.

Heat the olive oil in a large heavy-based frying pan. Add the red pepper and sauté for 5 minutes until just softened but not coloured. Add the potato cubes and cook for another 3 minutes until they are just beginning to colour. Tip in the peas and spinach and continue to cook for 2 minutes or until the spinach has wilted, stirring constantly.

Pour the egg mixture over the vegetables in the pan, then reduce the heat and cook the tortilla gently for about 8 minutes until the base is set. Place the pan directly under the grill for another 5 minutes until the top is set and lightly golden.

To Serve Cut the tortilla into wedges and arrange on serving plates warm or cold. Garnish with the coriander sprigs and lemon wedges, if liked, and serve with some salad on the side.

●Tip Be careful not to overcook the tortilla or it will become rubbery and unpleasant. Once it has cooked it should be golden brown on the outside but still succulent and moist in the middle.

Lamb and Apricot Pilaff

Serves 4

This pilaff is made from bulgar wheat, the light, moist, yet fluffy, nutty-tasting grain that is a traditional accompaniment to lamb in the Greek-Cypriot community. As the wheat grain has already been partially processed, that is, cracked by boiling, it absorbs moisture easily and therefore cooks quickly.

Ingredients

6oz / 175g bulgar wheat
3 tablespoons olive oil
6oz / 175g ready-to-eat dried apricots
1 bunch spring onions, trimmed and thinly sliced
2oz / 50g pine nuts
1 teaspoon ground cumin
2 tablespoons clear honey

1/4 pint / 150ml vegetable stock (from a stock cube is fine)
1 teaspoon ground coriander
1lb / 450g lamb leg steaks, trimmed and sliced
1/2 teaspoon ground paprika
2 teaspoons chopped fresh coriander
salt and freshly ground black pepper
crusty bread, to serve

Method Place the bulgar wheat in a heatproof bowl and cover with boiling water. Leave to stand for 30 minutes to allow the grains to swell, then drain and season with one teaspoon of salt. Set aside.

Heat two tablespoons of the olive oil in a large pan with a lid and cook the apricots, spring onions and the pine nuts for 4 minutes or until the spring onions are softened and the pine nuts are lightly toasted, stirring constantly.

Tip the drained bulgar wheat into the pan with the cumin, honey, stock and half of the ground coriander. Cover and cook for 3 minutes to allow the flavours to combine. Remove from the heat and tip back into a serving bowl. Season to taste. Cover with clingfilm to keep warm and set aside to allow the flavours to develop.

Meanwhile, place the lamb slices in a bowl. Add the paprika and the remaining ground coriander, then mix well to coat. Heat the remaining tablespoon of olive oil in a heavy-based frying pan and add the coated lamb slices. Stir-fry over a high heat for 6-8 minutes until just tender and lightly golden.

To Serve Stir the fresh coriander into the bulgar wheat with the stir-fried lamb and mix well to combine. Divide among warmed serving bowls and hand around some crusty bread.

● Tip The bulgar wheat mixture can be used immediately or will keep happily in the fridge for up to two days covered with clingfilm. Simply reheat on high in the microwave for a couple of minutes when needed.

Balsamic and Honey-Glazed Chicken Bake

Serves 4

This chicken bake is easy to make and perfect for a cold winter's night. If you can leave the chicken to marinate for 24 hours the flavour is even better, otherwise cooking it on the bed of vegetables is a great way to keep the chicken succulent.

Ingredients
4 skinless chicken breast fillets
2 carrots, cut into cubes
1 celeriac, well trimmed and cut into cubes
10oz / 300g baby new potatoes, halved
1 tablespoon olive oil
1 tablespoon chopped fresh parsley

For the Marinade
5 tablespoon clear honey
1 tablespoon wholegrain mustard
1 garlic clove, crushed
1 teaspoon freshly grated root ginger
2 tablespoons balsamic vinegar
2 tablespoons Worcestershire sauce

1 tablespoon fresh lemon juice
salt and freshly ground black pepper
lightly dressed green salad, to serve

Method To make the marinade, place the honey in a shallow non-metallic dish with the mustard, garlic, ginger, balsamic vinegar, Worcestershire sauce and lemon juice, stirring to combine. Add the chicken fillets, turning to coat and then cover with clingfilm. Chill for at least 6 hours or overnight in the fridge if time allows.

Preheat the oven to 220C/450F/Gas 7. Plunge the carrots, celeriac and baby potatoes into a pan of boiling salted water and simmer for 7 minutes until almost but not quite tender. Drain and quickly refresh, then tip into an ovenproof dish.

Heat the oil in a large heavy-based griddle pan over a high heat. Add the chicken fillets skin-side down, shaking off any excess marinade and cook for 1 minute, then turn over and cook for another minute until just seared on both sides. Brush the chicken with the remaining marinade and arrange on the bed of vegetables. Bake for 12-15 minutes or until chicken is cooked and nicely glazed and the vegetables are heated through.

To Serve Scatter the parsley over the chicken and vegetables and take the dish to the table. Serve with a bowl of green salad.

Tip To prepare the celeriac, cut off the top and bottom and then cut it into quarters. Using a small sharp knife, peel away the thick, knobbly skin and cut the remainder into even-sized cubes.

Mega Beefburgers

Serves 4

These beefburgers would also be delicious served with my Spicy Potato Wedges (page 19). If the sun is shining, cook them on a barbie, otherwise a griddle pan also works fine.

Ingredients

1 red pepper
2lb / 900g lean minced beef
1 onion, finely chopped
1 tablespoon sweet chilli sauce
1 egg, beaten
1 tablespoon freshly grated Parmesan
1oz / 25g fresh white breadcrumbs

1 tablespoon chopped fresh thyme and parsley
1 teaspoon Dijon mustard
2 tablespoons olive oil
4 slices Cheddar (such as Dubliner)
1 red onion, thinly sliced
4 hamburger buns, split in half
1oz / 25g rocket

2 ripe vine tomatoes, sliced
4 tablespoons mayonnaise
salt and freshly ground black pepper
tomato relish, to serve (shop-bought or homemade page 11)

Method Preheat the oven to 220C/425F/Gas 7. Place the pepper on a baking sheet and roast for 20-25 minutes or until the skin is blackened and blistered, and the flesh has softened. Once it is cool enough to handle, peel away the skin and discard with the stalks and seeds, then finely dice the flesh.

Place the diced red pepper in a bowl with the minced beef, onion, sweet chilli sauce, egg, Parmesan, breadcrumbs, herbs and mustard. Season to taste and divide into four even-sized portions then, using slightly wetted hands, shape into patties that are about 1in / 2.5cm thick. Cover and chill for at least 15 minutes and up to 1 hour to allow the burgers to firm up.

Preheat the grill. Heat the olive oil in a large frying pan and cook the burgers for 4-5 minutes on each side for medium, or give them another couple of minutes if you prefer your burgers well done. Transfer to a warm plate and place a cheese slice on top of each one, then leave to rest.

Add the red onion to the frying pan and sauté for 5 minutes until softened and lightly coloured around the edges. Arrange the split hamburger buns on a grill rack and toast under the grill.

To Serve Arrange the bottoms of the toasted buns on warmed serving plates and cover with the rocket and tomato slices, then place a cheese-topped burger on each one. Scatter over the sautéed red onion, then smear the tops of the toasted buns with the mayonnaise and place to the side. Serve with the tomato relish on the side.

● Tip Canned pimentos, otherwise known as sweet, piquant red peppers, would also work perfectly well in the burgers. Any leftovers keep in the fridge for up to two weeks, and you could use them to liven up a salad, or for my Red Pepper Hummus (page 85).

Trout and Baby Spinach Linguine

Serves 4

Sometimes the meals that are quick and easy are best, and the ones that you return to time and again. This is a brilliant healthy supper that's ready in less than 20 minutes from start to finish!

Ingredients
14oz / 400g linguine pasta
10oz / 300g large trout, cleaned, filleted
into four pieces and skinned
1 teaspoon olive oil
1 tablespoon fresh lime juice
2oz / 50g baby spinach leaves
6 spring onions, trimmed and thinly sliced

For the Dressing
4fl oz / 120ml extra virgin olive oil
1 tablespoon fresh lemon juice
$3^1/_2$ fl oz / 100ml freshly squeezed orange juice
1 teaspoon Dijon mustard
1 teaspoon snipped fresh chives
1 tablespoon finely diced red onion
salt and freshly ground black pepper
crusty bread, to serve

Method Preheat the grill to high. To make the dressing, place the olive oil in a small bowl with the lemon juice, orange juice, mustard, chives and onion. Whisk together until emulsified and then season to taste.

Plunge the linguine into a large pan of boiling salted water, stir once and cook for 8-10 minutes until *al dente*.

Lightly brush trout with the olive oil, season all over and arrange on the grill rack, then cook for 6-8 minutes, turning once and sprinkling with the lime juice half way through cooking.

Place the spinach in a bowl and add the spring onions and half of the dressing. Gently toss to combine, then set aside and allow the flavours to combine.

To Serve Drain the linguine and divide among warmed serving plates. Arrange the trout fillets on top and drizzle over the remaining dressing. Hand around the crusty bread at the table.

● **Tip** Try using spaghetti or noodles for a change and, if you're not into trout, salmon or plaice would work just as well.

Tuna Niçoise

Serves 4

Tuna is the fillet steak of the fish world. It should be cooked lightly as overcooking will dry it out. It's definitely best to cook it on a really hot griddle pan or, if you're in an *al fresco* mood, sear it over hot coals.

Ingredients
8oz / 225g baby new potatoes
2 eggs
5oz / 150g French beans, trimmed
4 x 4oz / 100g fresh tuna steaks, each about 1in / 2.5cm thick
3 tablespoons olive oil
1 red onion, thinly sliced

1 garlic clove, crushed
4 small ripe vine tomatoes, quartered
8 fresh basil leaves
4oz / 100g pitted black olives
3 tablespoons balsamic vinegar
1 tablespoon snipped fresh chives
salt and freshly ground black pepper
crusty bread, to serve

Method Place the potatoes in a pan of boiling salted water, cover and simmer for 15-18 minutes until just tender. Drain and leave to cool completely, then cut into slices and place in a bowl.

Place the eggs in a small pan and just cover with boiling water, then cook for 8-10 minutes until hard-boiled. Drain and rinse under cold running water, then remove the shells and cut each egg into quarters. Plunge the French beans into a pan of boiling salted water and blanch for a minute or so, then drain and refresh under cold running water.

Heat a griddle pan until very hot. Add the tuna steaks and cook for 2-3 minutes on each side until browned but still pink in the centre. Remove from the heat and leave to rest for a couple of minutes.

Meanwhile, heat olive oil in large heavy-based frying pan. Add the red onion and garlic and gently sauté for 3-4 minutes until softened but not coloured. Add the tomatoes and continue to sauté for 2 minutes, then stir in the sliced cooked potatoes, blanched French beans, basil, olives and balsamic vinegar. Season to taste and toss to combine.

To Serve Divide the potato mixture among serving bowls and arrange the hard-boiled egg quarters and seared tuna steaks on top. Sprinkle with the chives and hand a basket of crusty bread around the table.

Tip Use salmon fillets, if you prefer, or canned tuna as a cheaper alternative.

Smoked Mackerel Fish Cakes with Chilli Mayonnaise

Serves 4

These oven-baked fish cakes are wonderful served with the chilli mayonnaise. Why not make double the quantity and freeze half for a later date?

Ingredients
10oz / 300g potatoes, cut into chunks
2oz / 50g fresh or frozen peas
8oz / 225g smoked mackerel fillets
1 red pepper, cored, seeded and finely chopped
2 spring onions, finely chopped
1 tablespoon rinsed diced capers

1 tablespoon chopped fresh dill
1 tablespoon snipped fresh chives
finely grated rind and juice of 1 lemon
4oz / 100g fresh white breadcrumbs
1 tablespoon chopped fresh parsley
2 eggs
plain flour, for dusting
2 tablespoons olive oil

For the Chilli Mayonnaise
8 tablespoons low-fat mayonnaise
1 tablespoon sweet chilli sauce
$1/2$ teaspoon snipped fresh chives
$1/2$ teaspoon fresh lemon juice
salt and freshly ground black pepper

Method Cook the potatoes in a pan of boiling salted water for 15-20 minutes until tender. Cook the peas for 3-4 minutes until tender, then drain and quickly refresh. Drain the cooked potatoes and mash until smooth.

Peel away the skin from the smoked mackerel fillets and discard, then flake the flesh into the mashed potatoes. Add the cooked peas, red pepper, spring onions, capers, dill, chives and lemon juice and rind. Season to taste and mix until well combined.

Mix together the breadcrumbs and parsley in a shallow dish. Break the eggs into a separate shallow dish, season and lightly beat. Divide the fish mixture into eight even-sized portions, then using floured hands, shape into patties. Dip each one into the beaten egg and then coat in the breadcrumbs. Chill for at least 15 minutes to allow the mixture to firm up or up to 24 hours is fine covered with clingfilm.

Preheat the oven to 190C/375F/Gas 5. Heat the olive oil in a large ovenproof frying pan. Add the fishcakes and cook for 1-2 minutes on each side until crisp and lightly golden, then transfer to the oven and continue to cook for another 8-10 minutes or until heated through and golden brown.

To make the chilli mayonnaise, place the mayonnaise in a bowl with the sweet chilli sauce, chives and lemon juice. Season to taste and mix well to combine.

To Serve Arrange the fish cakes on warmed serving plates with some of the chilli mayonnaise on the side.

Tip For an even lower-fat version of the chilli mayonnaise, replace half of the mayonnaise with yoghurt or fromage frais.

Beef Stir-Fry with Noodles

Serves 4

Another lovely balance of flavours and textures for a quick no-nonsense yet healthy, tasty supper. Why not try making this with different kinds of noodles such as udon or rice noodles?

Ingredients
8oz / 225g medium Chinese egg noodles
2 tablespoons toasted sesame oil
1 red chilli, seeded and thinly sliced
2 garlic cloves, sliced
1lb / 450g thin cut sirloin steak, trimmed and sliced

6oz / 175g pak choi, cut across into 1in / 2.5cm wide strips
6oz / 175g shitake mushrooms, sliced
4oz / 100g canned water chestnuts, drained and sliced
3^1/$_2$ fl oz /100ml chicken stock (from a cube is fine)

4 tablespoons oyster sauce
4 tablespoons teriyaki sauce
4 spring onions, thinly sliced

Method Plunge the noodles into a pan of boiling salted water, then remove from the heat and set aside for 4 minutes or according to packet instructions. Drain and toss in half of the sesame oil, then cover with clingfilm to keep warm and set aside.

Heat a wok or large frying pan until smoking hot. Add the remaining sesame oil and swirl around, then quickly add in the chilli and garlic. Stir fry for 20 seconds, then tip in the steak and stir fry for another 2-3 minutes until just tender and lightly browned.

Add the pak choi to the wok with the shitake mushrooms and water chestnuts. Stir fry for another 2-3 minutes until the mushrooms are tender, then stir in the chicken stock, oyster sauce and teriyaki sauce and bring to a simmer until slightly thickened and heated through.

To Serve Divide the beef stir-fry among warmed serving bowls and sprinkle with half of the spring onions. Place the noodles in separate warmed bowls and scatter with remaining spring onions.

Tip Sirloin steak is very lean, but there is fat around the top edge of each steak and marbled throughout the meat itself. You can trim off the fat around the edge, but the marbled fat gives the meat a lovely succulence and flavour. If you want your meat completely lean, choose fillet instead.

Charred Chicken with Herb Mash

Serves 4

This charred chicken has to be one of my favourite dishes – the acidity of the balsamic vinegar makes a wonderful marinade that helps to make the chicken beautifully tender.

Ingredients
4 x 6oz / 175g skinless chicken breast fillets
2 tablespoons clear honey
1 tablespoon balsamic vinegar
1 garlic clove, crushed
2 teaspoons wholegrain mustard
1 tablespoon fresh lemon juice
olive oil, for brushing

For the Herb Mash
1½lb / 675g potatoes, cut into chunks
2 tablespoons extra virgin olive oil
3fl oz / 75ml semi-skimmed milk
4 tablespoons chopped fresh mixed herbs
(such as chives, parsley and basil)
salt and freshly ground black pepper

steamed sugar snap peas
and French beans, to serve

Method To marinate the chicken, place the honey in a shallow non-metallic dish with the balsamic vinegar, garlic, mustard and lemon juice. Season to taste and mix until well combined. Add the chicken breast fillets, turning to coat and then cover with clingfilm and leave to marinate in the fridge for at least 15 minutes or up to 24 hours is best.

To make the herb mash, cook the potatoes in a pan of boiling salted water for 15-20 minutes until tender. Drain and mash until smooth. Place the olive oil in a small pan with the milk and bring to a simmer, then beat into the mashed potatoes with the herbs. Season to taste.

Heat a griddle pan until very hot. Brush with olive oil and add the marinated chicken breast fillets, presentation-side down and cook for 5-6 minutes, then turn over and cook for another 8 minutes or so until tender and lightly charred.

To Serve Spoon the herb mash into a piping bag with 1in / 2.5cm nozzle and pipe on to warmed serving plates. Place a griddled chicken fillet on each serving and arrange the sugar snap peas and French beans around the plates.

● **Tip** The longer the chicken is left to 'sleep' in the honey mixture the better the flavour and the more tender it becomes.

Grilled Lamb Pittas

Serves 4

Try serving these deliciously, succulent lamb-burgers with a minted yoghurt dip, made from 7fl oz / 200ml low-fat Greek yoghurt, a quarter cucumber that has been grated with the water squeezed out, a handful of shredded mint leaves and a crushed garlic clove.

Ingredients
1½ lb / 675g lean minced lamb
2 tablespoons chopped fresh parsley
1 tablespoon chopped fresh mint
1 small onion, finely chopped
1 garlic clove, crushed
1 egg

1 tablespoon sweet chilli sauce
4 small wholemeal pitta pockets
2oz / 50g wild rocket

For the Mint Salad
3 ripe vine tomatoes, sliced
1 red onion, thinly sliced

1 tablespoon chopped fresh mint
1 tablespoon extra virgin olive oil
1 tablespoon fresh lemon juice
salt and freshly ground black pepper
chopped fresh parsley, to garnish

Method Place the minced lamb in a large bowl with the parsley, mint, onion, garlic, egg and sweet chilli sauce. Mix together until well combined and then divide the mixture into twelve equal portions. Using wetted hands, shape into patties and then arrange on a baking sheet. Cover with clingfilm and chill for 30 minutes to allow the mixture to firm up.

Preheat the grill and the oven to 160C/325F/Gas 3. Arrange the patties on a grill rack and cook for 10 minutes or until cooked through and golden brown, turning once.

Meanwhile, wrap the pitta bread in foil and place in the oven for 5 minutes to warm through. To make mint salad, place the tomatoes, red onion, mint, olive oil and lemon juice in a bowl. Season to taste and toss gently to coat.

To Serve Remove the pitta breads from the oven and split open each pocket, then fill with the rocket, some mint salad and the lamb-burgers. Arrange on warmed serving plates and garnish with parsley.

Tip To ring in the changes, try using minced chicken or turkey – both are really lean and low in fat.

Baked Potatoes

Serves 4

The baked potato is undoubtedly the greatest standby meal. Choose a floury variety, such as Maris Piper, King Edward or Rooster and a 7oz / 200g specimen is the perfect size. I love mine with just a pinch of Maldon sea salt and a knob of butter, served with a crisp green salad; or if you're feeling more adventurous try some of the topping suggestions I have listed below.

Ingredients
4 baking potatoes
olive oil, for brushing

Method   Preheat the oven to 200C/400F/Gas 6. Prick the potatoes all over with a fork to allow the steam to escape. Place on a baking sheet and rub a little olive oil all over the skins. Bake for 1 hour or until soft when gently squeezed.

To Serve   Cut a deep cross in the cooked baked potato and, using a clean tea towel, gently press in the sides. Fluff up the flesh with a fork and serve at once.

TOPPING SUGGESTIONS

Bubbling Chicken Tikka Mix two tablespoons tikka paste with four tablespoons natural yoghurt. Add two skinless chicken breast fillets. Cover with clingfilm and leave marinade in fridge for 1 hour. Preheat grill and arrange the marinated chicken fillets on a grill rack, shaking off any excess marinade, then cook for 10-12 minutes until cooked through and tender, turning once. Leave to cool slightly, then roughly chop and place in a bowl. Add two tablespoons low-fat mayonnaise and one tablespoon chopped fresh coriander. Mix well to combine and season to taste, then spoon into baked potatoes to serve.

Smoked Bacon, Avocado and Red Onion Preheat the grill. Peel one ripe avocado, then cut in half, discard the stone and cut the flesh into bite-sized chunks. Place in a bowl and add a squeeze of lemon juice to prevent it discolouring. Arrange three rindless smoked bacon rashers on a grill rack and cook for a minute or two on each side, then leave to cool slightly before chopping. Add to the avocado with one finely diced small red onion and then stir in two tablespoons low-fat mayonnaise and one tablespoon chopped fresh parsley. Season to taste and spoon into baked potatoes. Serve with salad.

Tuna, Mushroom and Garlic Heat one tablespoon olive oil in a frying pan and sauté 4oz / 100g sliced button mushrooms with one crushed garlic clove for 5 minutes until tender. Season to taste and then stir in one tablespoon chopped fresh parsley, two tablespoons low-fat Greek yoghurt and 7oz / 200g drained can of tuna in brine. Mix well and use to fill baked potatoes to serve.

Cottage Cheese, Spinach and Sun-Dried Tomatoes Heat one tablespoon olive oil. Tip in 8oz / 225g baby spinach leaves and stir for a minute or so until wilted. Drain off any excess water and then mix in two tablespoons chopped sun-dried tomatoes, one tablespoon chopped fresh basil and two tablespoons low-fat cottage cheese. Season to taste and spoon into baked potatoes to serve.

Tofu and Vegetable Stir-Fry

Serves 4

Tofu is a white curd made from soya beans that is perfect for veggies. It is now available in large supermarkets or health food shops. Look out for it in the chilled cabinets but don't buy frozen as it tends to break up in stir-fries and is difficult to achieve a golden brown colour.

Ingredients
2 tablespoons dark soy sauce
2 tablespoons rice wine vinegar
1 tablespoon caster sugar
1 small red chilli, seeded and finely chopped
2 teaspoons Chinese five-spice powder
10oz / 300g packet firm tofu, drained and cut into chunks
2 tablespoons toasted sesame oil
1 red and 1 yellow pepper, cored, seeded and sliced

1 courgette, trimmed and sliced on the diagonal
6oz / 175g broccoli florets
7oz / 200g shitake mushrooms, trimmed and sliced
6oz / 175g Chinese cabbage, cored and shredded
2 teaspoons cornflour
4 tablespoons vegetable stock (from a cube is fine)
2 teaspoons toasted sesame seeds
steamed rice, to serve

Method Place the soy sauce in a shallow non-metallic dish and add the rice wine vinegar, sugar, chilli and Chinese five-spice powder. Mix well to combine and then stir in the tofu until well coated. Cover with clingfilm and marinate in the fridge for 2 hours.

Heat a wok or large frying pan and add half of the sesame oil. Drain the tofu, reserving the marinade and then stir-fry in batches for 2-3 minutes until golden brown. Transfer to a bowl and keep warm.

Add the remaining sesame oil to the wok and then tip in the red and yellow peppers, courgette, broccoli and shitake mushrooms. Stir fry for 3 minutes or until all of the vegetables are just tender.

Mix the cornflour with the stock and reserved marinade in a small bowl. Tip the Chinese cabbage into the wok and stir-fry until combined, then pour in the cornflour mixture, stirring to combine. Add the reserved tofu and continue to stir-fry for a minute or so until the sauce has thickened.

To Serve Scatter with sesame seeds and spoon into warmed serving bowls. Hand around a separate bowl of steamed rice at the table.

Tip To check and see if the vegetables are cooked, pierce them with the tip of a sharp knife - there should be no resistance and the vegetables should feel as soft as butter.

Barbecued Pork Ribs

Serves 4

Delicious lip-smacking ribs are hard to beat. Try to buy the meatiest, leanest ribs you can find and ask your butcher to cut them into individual ribs for you.

Ingredients
5lb / 2.25kg pork ribs
4 tablespoons pouring golden syrup
4 tablespoons tomato ketchup
3 tablespoons dark soy sauce
1 garlic clove, crushed
2 tablespoons sweet chilli sauce
2 tablespoons balsamic vinegar
1 tablespoon tomato puree

Method Preheat the oven to 200C/400F/Gas 6. Tip the pork ribs into a large roasting tin. Place the golden syrup in a bowl with the ketchup, soy sauce, garlic, sweet chilli sauce, balsamic vinegar and tomato puree. Stir until well combined.

Pour the golden syrup mixture over the ribs, give the tin a good shake and then baste the marinade over ribs until well covered. Roast for 1 hour and 10 minutes, basting every 10 minutes until completely tender and sticky. Remove from the oven and leave to cool slightly, then chop into several portions.

To Serve Arrange the ribs on warmed serving plates or on one large platter with finger bowls and plenty of napkins to hand for all those messy fingers!!

Tip If time allows, marinate the ribs in a shallow non-metal container covered with clingfilm in the fridge for anything up to two days to allow the flavours to penetrate the meat as much as possible.

Thai Green Curry

Serves 4

I'm really into the smooth, silky taste of this fragrant curry. Although Thai green curry paste is now readily available, I like to make my own, but that, of course, is entirely up to you.

Ingredients
1 tablespoon vegetable oil
4 skinless chicken breast fillets, cut into chunks
14oz / 400g can coconut milk
8oz / 225g can bamboo shoots, drained and rinsed
6oz / 175g green beans, trimmed
3 tablespoons shredded basil leaves, plus extra leaves to garnish

For the Thai Green Curry Paste
2 green chillies, seeded and sliced
2 lemon-grass stalks, outer leaves removed and sliced
3 tablespoons chopped fresh coriander
1 teaspoon coriander seeds
1 teaspoon black peppercorns
1 teaspoon cumin seeds
1 teaspoon ground turmeric

2 shallots, chopped
3 garlic cloves, peeled
1 teaspoon freshly grated root ginger
finely grated rind and juice of 1 lime
$1/2$ teaspoon salt
2 tablespoons Thai fish sauce (nam pla)
Thai fragrant rice to serve

Method To make the Thai green curry paste, place the chillies in a food processor or liquidiser with the lemon-grass, fresh coriander, coriander seeds, peppercorns, cumin seeds, turmeric, shallots, garlic, ginger, lime rind and juice, salt and Thai fish sauce. Add six tablespoons of water and blend to a smooth paste. Transfer to a sterilised screw-topped jar.

Heat the oil in a wok or large pan. Add the chicken and stir fry for 5-6 minutes until golden brown. Add three tablespoons of the Thai green curry paste (the remainder can be used at another time) and stir for 30 seconds, then pour in the coconut milk and add the bamboo shoots and green beans. Bring to the boil, then reduce the heat and simmer gently for 15 minutes until the chicken is cooked through and the beans are tender. Stir in shredded basil.

To Serve Ladle the Thai green curry into warmed serving bowls and garnish with the basil leaves. Serve separate bowls of the Thai fragrant rice.

Tip This recipe for the Thai green curry paste will keep in the fridge for up to 1 week, as you'll need only three tablespoons for the recipe. Freeze the remainder for up to 1 month in the screw-topped jar.

Oriental Pork Fillet with Mixed Peppers

Serves 4

Pork fillet is not only economical to buy, but it is also very lean and therefore low in fat. Here it is marinated and served with a quick Oriental-style noodle stir-fry.

Ingredients

4 ripe vine tomatoes, roughly chopped
2 garlic cloves, peeled
1 teaspoon freshly grated root ginger
2 red chillies, seeded and chopped
large pinch ground cinnamon
1 teaspoon Chinese five-spice powder

3 tablespoons dark soy sauce
3 tablespoons dark muscovado sugar
2 x 12oz / 350g pork fillets, well trimmed
8oz / 225g medium Chinese egg noodles
1 tablespoon toasted sesame oil
1 red, 1 yellow and 1 green pepper,
cored, seeded and finely sliced

4 spring onions, thinly sliced
fresh parsley sprigs, to garnish
(optional)

Method Place the tomatoes in a food processor or liquidiser with the garlic, ginger, chillies, cinnamon, Chinese five-spice, soy sauce and sugar. Blend until smooth and then transfer to a pan with a spatula. Bring to the boil and boil fast for 5 minutes until you have achieved a thick paste, stirring occasionally. Remove from the heat and leave to cool completely.

Place the pork fillets in a shallow non-metallic dish and pour over them the cooled tomato paste, then rub all over with your hands. Cover with clingfilm and leave to marinate in the fridge for at least 2 hours or overnight is best.

Preheat the oven to 200C/400F/Gas 6. Place the pork fillets on a rack set over a roasting tin and bake for 30 minutes or until cooked through and tender, brushing every 10 minutes or so with the marinade. Leave to rest in a warm place for 5 minutes.

Meanwhile, heat a wok or large frying pan until very hot. Plunge the noodles into a pan of boiling salted water and then remove from the heat. Set aside for 4 minutes or according to packet instructions until cooked through, then drain and cover with clingfilm to keep warm. Add the sesame oil to the wok and then tip in the peppers. Stir-fry over a high heat for 3 minutes until just tender and then tip in the spring onions. Toss well to combine and continue to cook until heated through.

To Serve Slice the pork fillets on the diagonal and arrange on warmed serving plates with the mixed peppers. Garnish with the parsley sprigs, if liked, and serve with a separate bowl of noodles.

● **Tip** Chinese five-spice is a mixture of anise pepper, cassia, fennel seed, star anise and cloves, all ground to a fine powder. It has a powerful anise flavour and aroma, bordering on liquorice.

Gingered Chicken Parcels

Serves 4

These individual Oriental-inspired parcels should be served unopened to your guests for the maximum effect. However, I also find making one family-size parcel very handy and it still gives excellent results – you'll just need to increase the cooking time by another 5 to 10 minutes.

Ingredients
2 x 5oz / 150g skinless chicken breast fillets, thinly sliced
2 garlic cloves, finely chopped
1 teaspoon freshly grated root ginger
1 small red chilli, seeded and sliced
2 tablespoons dark soy sauce
2 tablespoons oyster sauce
handful fresh coriander leaves

2 carrots, thinly sliced on the diagonal
1 red and 1 yellow pepper, cored, seeded and cut into diamond shapes
6oz / 175g sugar snap peas
8oz / 225g can water chestnuts, drained, rinsed and thinly sliced
4 spring onions, sliced on the diagonal
Chinese egg noodles or plain boiled rice, to serve

Method Place the chicken in a non-metallic dish with the garlic, ginger, chilli, soy sauce, oyster sauce and coriander leaves. Mix well to combine, then cover with clingfilm and leave to marinate in the fridge for at least 30 minutes or up to 24 hours is best.

Preheat the oven to 180C/350F/Gas 4. Add the carrots to the chicken mixture with the red and yellow peppers, sugar snap peas, spring onions and water chestnuts. Mix well to combine.

Cut out 4 x 10in / 25cm squares of greaseproof paper or non-stick baking parchment. Divide the chicken mixture between the four squares, spooning into the centre of each one. Fold the paper over the chicken from all four sides to totally enclose the filling and then seal the edges together with a double fold, making sure there is plenty of room for expansion. Place the parcels on a large baking sheet and bake for 20-25 minutes or until the parcels have puffed up, which indicates the chicken is cooked through and tender.

To Serve Arrange a parcel on each warmed serving plate and hand around some noodles or rice separately to serve.

Tip Although tinfoil mightn't look as attractive, it also works well for the parcels and should slightly shorten the cooking time.

Beef Satay

Serves 4

Don't let the long list of ingredients put you off this dish – it really is worth the effort and is actually very simple to prepare. My brother Kenneth, who loves cooking, has very kindly passed this recipe on to me.

Ingredients
½ teaspoon Chinese five-spice powder
2 tablespoons pineapple juice
2 tablespoons light soy sauce
2 garlic cloves, crushed
2 teaspoons caster sugar
1lb / 450g rump or sirloin steak, trimmed and cut into thin strips

For the Satay Sauce
1 carrot, grated
1 tablespoon rice wine vinegar
1 tablespoon vegetable oil
1 onion, diced
3 garlic cloves, crushed
1 teaspoon freshly grated root ginger
1 red and 1 green pepper, cored, seeded and cut into strips

1 tablespoon tomato puree
3½fl oz / 100ml sweet chilli sauce
3½fl oz / 100ml dark soy sauce
14oz / 400g can coconut milk
4oz / 100g crunchy peanut butter
3oz / 75g cashew nuts (optional)
Thai fragrant rice, to serve
fresh coriander sprigs, to garnish

Method To make the marinade, place the Chinese five-spice powder in a shallow non-metallic dish with the pineapple juice, soy sauce, garlic and caster sugar. Mix until well combined and then tip in the beef, turning to coat. Cover with clingfilm and leave to marinate in the fridge for at least 2 hours or up to 24 hours is best.

To make the satay sauce, place the carrot in a bowl and pour over the rice wine vinegar. Cover with clingfilm and set aside for 1 hour to allow the flavours to combine.

Heat the oil in a heavy-based pan. Add the onion, garlic, ginger, red and green peppers, then sauté gently for 5 minutes until softened but not coloured. Add the tomato puree with the sweet chilli sauce, soy sauce, coconut milk, peanut butter and three tablespoons of water. Stir well to combine, then bring to the boil and simmer for 10-15 minutes until slightly reduced and thickened, stirring occasionally. Stir in the soaked carrots, and cashew nuts, if using. Season to taste, remove from the heat and leave to cool.

Preheat a large griddle pan until very hot. Thread the marinated steak on to 8 x 8in / 20cm bamboo skewers. Add to the heated pan and cook for 8-10 minutes, brushing with the remaining marinade and turning occasionally until cooked through and lightly charred.

To Serve Arrange the satay skewers on warmed serving plates with some of the Thai fragrant rice and pour over some of the satay sauce, or serve separately in small bowls on the side.

Tip   Pineapple juice is now readily available in supermarkets in cartons and acts as the most natural, wonderful tenderiser for meat.

Melting Turkey Quesadillas

Serves 4

A classic Mexican restaurant dish, simple, with lovely tastes and textures, and served with an easy tomato salsa for dipping – delicious!

Ingredients
4 tablespoons olive oil
1 red onion, thinly sliced
1 small yellow and 1 small green pepper, cored, seeded and sliced
8oz / 225g turkey breast fillets, cut into strips
1 1/4oz / 35g packet fajita seasoning mix
4 large soft flour tortilla wraps

9oz / 250g mozzarella cheese
4 tablespoons refried beans (from a can)

For the Tomato Salsa
1 tablespoon olive oil
1 onion, finely chopped
1 garlic clove, crushed
1 red chilli, seeded and finely chopped

14oz / 400g can chopped tomatoes
1/2 teaspoon sugar
pinch hot chilli powder
salt and freshly ground black pepper
lightly dressed rocket salad, to serve

Method To make the tomato salsa, heat the oil in a pan. Add the onion, garlic and chilli and sauté gently for 3-5 minutes until completely softened but not coloured. Add the tomatoes, sugar and chilli powder and simmer for another 10-15 minutes or until slightly reduced and thickened. Season to taste and leave to cool.

Heat one tablespoon of the olive oil in a large frying pan or wok. Add the red onion, yellow and green peppers and stir fry for 5 minutes until softened and tender. Tip into a bowl. Add another tablespoon of oil to the pan and then tip in the turkey strips. Sprinkle with the fajita seasoning mix, stirring to combine. Stir-fry for 4-6 minutes until cooked through and lightly golden. Return the onion and peppers to the pan and continue to cook for another minute or so until well combined.

Meanwhile, heat a separate large frying pan. Add a soft flour tortilla wrap and heat for 20 seconds, turning once until soft and pliable but not coloured. Repeat with the remaining flour tortillas and stack them up on a warm plate.

Lay a softened flour tortilla wrap on a clean board. Spoon a quarter of the turkey mixture down the centre, cover with a quarter of the mozzarella and then add a tablespoon of the refried beans. Fold up the tortilla, tucking in the ends to form a parcel, then secure with a cocktail stick. Repeat with the remaining tortillas until you have four parcels in total.

Wipe out the large frying pan and then use to heat the remaining two tablespoons of olive oil. Fry the tortillas for 3-4 minutes, turning once until heated through and golden brown – you may have to do this in batches.

To Serve Arrange the quesadillas on warmed serving plates with some of the rocket salad and add a small dish of the tomato salsa on the side for dipping.

●Tip   There are a number of ways to make the flour tortillas soft enough for rolling: pop them on a hot frying or griddle pan, or alternatively microwave on high between dampened sheets of kitchen paper for about 30 seconds.

Sesame Prawn Toasts with Oriental Dipping Sauce

Makes 20

This recipe is very easy to make as everything gets blitzed in a food processor, spread on bread and sprinkled with sesame seeds. You can eat them as starters, snacks or canapés. I like them with the Oriental dipping sauce but they are also delicious with just a squeeze of lime.

Ingredients
8oz / 225g peeled raw prawns, cleaned
1 egg white
1 teaspoon cornflour
1 teaspoon fresh lemon juice
1 teaspoon dark soy sauce
1 teaspoon sweet chilli sauce
1 small garlic clove, crushed
1/2 teaspoon freshly grated root ginger

1 teaspoon Dijon mustard
5 slices white bread
3 tablespoons sesame seeds
vegetable oil, for deep-frying

For the Oriental Dipping Sauce
6 tablespoons dark soy sauce
3 tablespoons clear honey
1 teaspoon light muscovado sugar

1 teaspoon toasted sesame oil
1 red bird's eye chilli, seeded and thinly sliced
1 teaspoon finely grated fresh root ginger
1 small lemon-grass stalk, outer leaves removed and finely chopped
lightly dressed mixed salad leaves, to serve

Method
To make the Oriental dipping sauce, place the soy sauce in a small pan with the honey, sugar, sesame oil, chilli, ginger and lemon-grass. Place over a gentle heat and allow to infuse for 5 minutes, stirring occasionally. Remove from the heat and leave to stand for 20 minutes. This will allow the flavours to develop, then strain into a sterilised jar or bottle - it will keep happily in the fridge for up to 2 weeks.

Place the prawns in a food processor or liquidiser with the egg white, cornflour, lemon juice, soy sauce, sweet chilli sauce, garlic, ginger and mustard. Blend to a smooth paste.

Spread the prawn paste over the bread and sprinkle a teaspoon or two of the sesame seeds over each slice, pressing them down gently with your fingertips. Arrange on a baking sheet, then cover with clingfilm and chill until needed.

Preheat the oil to 180C/350F in a deep-fat fryer or a deep-sided pan. Deep-fry the toasts for about 1-1½ minutes on each side or until golden. Drain on kitchen paper and then cut off the crusts and cut each slice into four triangles.

To Serve
Arrange the sesame prawn toasts on warmed serving plates or one large platter with small bowls of the Oriental dipping sauce.

Tip The bread for this recipe is best 1-2 days old. This allows it to dry out slightly and move on from the doughy texture.

Sausage Rolls with Sesame Seeds

Makes about 40

I just never seem to be able to make enough of these. Fortunately, they take just minutes to make and seconds to demolish. You have been warned! Don't forget to hand around napkins for those greasy fingers.

Ingredients
1oz / 25g butter
2 tablespoons finely diced onion
3 eggs
1lb / 450g sausage meat (good quality)
2 tablespoons sweet chilli sauce
1 tablespoon chopped fresh basil

1 tablespoon cream
8oz / 225g ready-rolled puff pastry, thawed if frozen
plain flour, for dusting
2 tablespoons sesame seeds
butter, for greasing
salt and freshly ground black pepper

Method Preheat the oven to 220C/425F/Gas 7. Melt the butter in a frying pan and sauté the onion for about 5 minutes until softened but not coloured. Remove from the heat and leave to cool.

Break two of the eggs into a food processor or liquidiser and add the sausage meat, sweet chilli sauce, basil and cream. Blend for 2 minutes until smooth, then scrape out into a bowl with a spatula and stir in the cooked onions. Season to taste and place the mixture in a piping bag with 1in / 2.5cm plain nozzle.

Beat the remaining egg in a small bowl with a pinch of salt and set aside for glazing. Place the puff pastry on a lightly floured surface and cut into four strips, each measuring 10in / 25cm x 3in / 7.5cm. Pipe the sausage meat mixture down the centre of each pastry strip and brush along one long edge with a little of the beaten egg. Roll up to enclose and press down the edges firmly to seal.

Brush the sausage rolls with the remaining beaten egg and sprinkle lightly with the sesame seeds. Cut into 1in / 2.5cm lengths and arrange on lightly buttered large baking sheets. Bake for 15 minutes or until crisp and golden.

To Serve Arrange the sausage rolls on a warmed serving platter and hand around with napkins.

●Tip These sausage rolls can be frozen uncooked for up to one month. Layer up between sheets of non-stick baking parchment in a plastic rigid container and secure with a lid before freezing. Increase the cooking time by about 10 minutes if cooking straight from frozen.

Smoked Salmon and Cream Cheese on Crackers

Makes about 20

These canapés literally take minutes to make and the smoked salmon mixture can be made up to one week in advance and kept covered with clingfilm in the fridge. The crackers can be chosen according to personal preference and are a useful standby to keep in the cupboard.

Ingredients
12 oz / 350g full fat cream cheese
8oz / 225g smoked salmon, finely chopped
1 tablespoon sweet chilli sauce
1 teaspoon chopped fresh parsley

1 teaspoon fresh lemon juice
5oz / 150g packet Ritz or mini Tuc crackers
salt and freshly ground black pepper
fresh chervil sprigs, to garnish

Method Place the cream cheese in a bowl with the smoked salmon, sweet chilli sauce, parsley and lemon juice. Using a wooden spoon, beat until smooth and then season to taste. Spoon into a piping bag fitted with a ½ in / 1cm fluted nozzle and place in the fridge for at least 30 minutes and up to 24 hours to firm up.

To Serve Pipe the smoked salmon cream cheese on to the crackers and arrange on a large serving platter. Garnish with the chervil sprigs.

● Tip Don't be tempted to pipe the smoked salmon mixture on the crackers too soon or the biscuits will go soggy.

Chicken Dippers with Carrot and Cucumber Raita

Makes about 20

Kids just love these chicken dippers and they taste so much nicer than shop-bought nuggets. They can also be cooked in a deep-fat fryer but obviously it's much healthier to bake them in the oven.

Ingredients

5oz / 150g fresh white breadcrumbs
1 tablespoon sesame seeds
1 tablespoon chopped fresh parsley
2 tablespoons medium curry powder
2 tablespoons plain flour
2 eggs, beaten
1lb / 450g skinless chicken breast fillets
olive oil, for greasing

For the Carrot and Cucumber Raita

9fl oz / 250ml low fat natural yoghurt
2 garlic cloves, crushed
1 teaspoon fresh lemon juice
1 small carrot, grated
1/2 small cucumber, halved, seeded and grated
salt and freshly ground black pepper
fresh coriander sprigs, to garnish

Method Preheat the oven to 180C/350F/Gas 4. Place the breadcrumbs in a food processor or liquidiser with the sesame seeds, parsley and curry powder. Blend for 2 minutes until well combined and then tip into a shallow dish.

Place the flour on a flat plate and season to taste. Place the eggs in a shallow dish. Cut the chicken fillets into about 20 even-sized strips and then toss each one into seasoned flour, shaking off any excess.

Dip the coated chicken strips into the beaten egg and then coat in the breadcrumbs. Arrange on an oiled large baking sheet, well spaced apart. Bake for 10 minutes or until cooked through and until golden brown.

To make the carrot and cucumber raita, place the yoghurt in a bowl and stir in the garlic, lemon juice, carrot and cucumber. Season to taste.

To Serve Stick each chicken dipper with a coriander leaf on the end of a 6in / 15cm bamboo skewer and then arrange on a warmed serving platter with the bowl of the carrot and cucumber raita to the side.

● Tip These chicken dippers can be prepared the day before they are needed and just popped into the oven when you are ready for them. The raita can also be made the day before, covered with clingfilm and kept chilled until you are ready to serve.

Pizza Bites

FOR THE PIZZA DOUGH   *Makes 20 pizza bites.*

Ingredients $^1/_2$ oz / 15g dried yeast • 1 teaspoon caster sugar • $3^1/_2$ fl oz / 100ml warm water • 8oz / 225g strong bread flour, plus extra for dusting • $^1/_2$ teaspoon salt • 1 teaspoon olive oil, plus extra for greasing

Method   Mix the yeast and sugar in a bowl with a little of the water. Leave for 5 minutes in a warm place. Sieve the flour and salt into a bowl, make a well in the centre and then mix in the yeast mixture, olive oil and the remaining water until you have achieved a firm dough. Knead on a floured surface for about 5 minutes, then tip into an oiled bowl, cover with a tea towel and leave to prove in a warm place for 15-20 minutes or until doubled in size.

Tip the dough out on to a floured surface and knead again for a couple of minutes until smooth and pliable, then divide into 20 pieces. Shape each piece of dough into a 2in / 5cm round, leaving it slightly thicker around the edges to form a rim. Cover with one of the topping suggestions listed below.

TOPPING SUGGESTIONS   *Each makes 20 pizza bites.*

Tomato, Chilli and Goat's Cheese Pizza Bites Preheat the oven to 220C/425F/Gas 7. Mix two teaspoons chopped fresh thyme in a shallow non-metallic dish with one tablespoon sweet chilli sauce and $3^1/_2$ fl oz / 100ml olive oil. Add 6oz / 175g diced goat's cheese, turning until completely coated. Cover with clingfilm and leave to marinate for 20 minutes. Meanwhile, melt 1oz / 25g butter in a pan and sweat six finely chopped spring onions for a few minutes until softened but not coloured. Add two finely chopped ripe vine tomatoes and season to taste. Spread the tomato mixture on to one quantity of the pizza bases and arrange on an oiled baking sheet. Arrange the marinated goat's cheese on top and bake for 10-12 minutes until cooked through and lightly golden.

Leek, Bacon and Red Onion Pizza Bites Preheat the oven to 220C/425F/Gas 7. Place 1oz / 25g butter and one tablespoon olive oil in a pan. Add two diced rindless smoked bacon rashers, one finely chopped red onion, two thinly sliced leeks and sweat for 10 minutes until softened but not coloured. Season to taste. Spread 7oz / 200g crème fraîche on to one quantity of the pizza bases. Sprinkle the leek mixture on top with 2oz / 50g freshly grated Parmesan. Finish with one tablespoon chopped fresh thyme and plenty of black pepper. Bake for 10-12 minutes until cooked through and lightly golden.

Wild Mushroom and Ricotta Pizza Bites Preheat the oven to 220C/425F/Gas 7. Drain 2 x 14oz / 400g cans whole plum tomatoes and chop roughly the flesh, then tip into a bowl. Season with salt and add two tablespoons olive oil and six torn fresh basil leaves. Heat another two tablespoons olive oil in a frying pan and sauté 9oz / 250g sliced mixed mushrooms, such as oyster, chestnuts and chanterelle with one crushed garlic clove for about 5 minutes until tender and lightly browned. Spread the tomato mixture over one quantity of the pizza bases and scatter the sautéed mushrooms on top. Cover with 8oz / 225g ricotta. Bake for 10-12 minutes until cooked through and lightly golden. Garnish with shredded fresh basil leaves.

Rocket, Mozzarella and Pine Nut Pizza Preheat the oven to 220C/425F/Gas 7. Chop $1^1/_2$ lb / 675g cherry tomatoes and place in a pan with one tablespoon olive oil. Add one crushed garlic clove and one teaspoon chopped fresh oregano and then simmer for 3-4 minutes until slightly reduced and thickened. Spoon the cherry tomato mixture on to one quantity of the pizza bases and scatter 9oz / 250g diced buffalo mozzarella on top with one tablespoon toasted pine nuts. Bake for 10-12 minutes until cooked through and lightly golden. Sprinkle with a handful of wild chopped rocket. Drizzle over a little extra virgin olive oil.

To Serve   Arrange the pizza bites on a large warmed serving platter.

Sticky Beef Skewers

Makes 20

It is important to soak the bamboo skewers you need for this recipe for at least half an hour before using them, otherwise they'll burn under the grill. However, if you do forget – all's not lost, simply cook them on a griddle pan, problem solved!

Ingredients

2 garlic cloves, crushed
3 tablespoons clear honey
1 tablespoon Worcestershire sauce
1 tablespoon dark soy sauce

1 tablespoon balsamic vinegar
1 teaspoon wholegrain mustard
2lb / 900g sirloin steak, trimmed and cut into thin strips
garlic and chive mayonnaise, to serve (see tip below)

Method Place the garlic in a shallow non-metallic dish and add the honey, Worcestershire sauce, soy sauce, balsamic vinegar and mustard. Mix until well combined. Thread the sirloin strips on to 20 x 4in / 10cm soaked bamboo skewers and add the marinade, turning to coat. Cover with clingfilm and chill for at least 6 hours or up to 24 hours in fridge.

Preheat the grill. Drain the beef skewers, reserving any remaining marinade and arrange on a grill rack. Cook for 8-10 minutes, turning once and brushing regularly with the rest of the marinade until cooked through and well caramelised.

To Serve Arrange the sticky beef skewers on a large warmed serving platter around a bowl of garlic and chive mayonnaise for dipping.

● Tip To make your own garlic and chive mayonnaise, simply stir two crushed garlic cloves and two tablespoons snipped fresh chives into $1/4$ pint / 150ml shop-bought or homemade mayonnaise.

Dips with Chips

There's no doubt that whether you are planning an informal family lunch or dinner for friends everyone likes to have something to nibble on whilst you are putting the finishing touches to the food. It can be as simple as layering up tortilla chips, pretzels and different kinds of crisps in a zig-zag pattern in pretty vases. I also like to dot bowls of dips around the room and have given a couple of my favourite suggestions below. Just remember it does not have to be difficult to be effective.

Guacamole   *Makes about ¹/₂ pint / 300ml*

Ingredients 2 ripe avocados • finely grated rind and juice of 2 limes • 1 small red onion, finely chopped
1 red chilli, seeded and finely chopped • 2 ripe tomatoes, peeled, seeded and diced • 1 garlic clove, crushed
2 tablespoons chopped fresh coriander • salt and freshly ground black pepper • tortilla chips, to serve

Method Cut the avocados in half and remove the stones, then scoop out the flesh into a bowl. Mash until smooth and add the lime rind and juice, red onion, chilli, tomatoes, garlic and coriander. Mix well to combine and season to taste.

To Serve Transfer the guacamole to a serving bowl and have a separate bowl of tortilla chips for dipping.

Chilli Jam   *Makes about ¹/₂ pint / 300ml*

Ingredients 2 tablespoons olive oil • 2 onions, diced • 2 red peppers, cored, seeded and diced • 1 garlic clove, crushed
1 red chilli, seeded and finely chopped • 1 tablespoon tomato puree • 1 tablespoon balsamic vinegar
2oz / 50g light muscovado sugar • 4 ripe tomatoes, diced • dash dark soy sauce • Kettle chips, to serve

Method Heat the olive oil in a heavy-based pan. Add the onions, red peppers and garlic and sauté for 2 minutes until just beginning to soften. Stir in the chilli and tomato puree and cook for 3 minutes, stirring to combine. Stir in the balsamic vinegar, sugar, tomatoes and soy sauce and pour in enough water to cover. Simmer for 15-20 minutes until well reduced and thickened, stirring occasionally. Remove from the heat and leave to cool completely, then tip into a food processor or liquidiser and blend to a puree. Pass through a sieve set over a bowl and season to taste.

To Serve Transfer the chilli jam to a serving bowl and have a separate bowl of Kettle chips for dipping.

Roasted Red Pepper Hummus   *Makes about ¹/₂ pint / 300ml*

Ingredients 1 garlic clove, chopped • 1 red chilli, seeded and roughly chopped • handful fresh coriander leaves •
2 canned pimentos, roughly chopped (or from a jar) • 14oz / 400g can chickpeas, drained and rinsed • juice of 1 lime
2 tablespoons toasted sesame oil • salt and freshly ground black pepper • Pringles, to serve

Method Place the garlic, chilli and coriander in a food processor or liquidiser and blend until finely chopped. Add the pimentos and chickpeas and blend again until well combined. With the motor running, pour in the lime juice and drizzle in the sesame oil to make a fairly smooth puree. Season to taste.

To Serve Transfer the roasted red pepper hummus to a serving bowl and have a separate bowl of Pringles for dipping.

Sweet Onion and Goat's Cheese Bruschetta

Serves 8-10

Brushetta make delicious simple nibbles and can look very impressive laid out on platters. Experiment with other toppings such as Parma ham and rocket or try my Guacamole (page 85) or Red Pepper Hummus (page 85). Whichever ones you decide to serve, I think they are perfect to hand around with drinks at any type of celebration.

Ingredients
5 tablespoons olive oil
3 red onions, thinly sliced
8oz / 225g ready-to-eat dried figs, finely chopped
2 garlic cloves, crushed
1/4 pint / 150ml red wine
2 tablespoons balsamic vinegar

1 teaspoon caster sugar
1 tablespoon chopped fresh thyme
1 French stick, thinly sliced on the diagonal
1lb / 450g goat's cheese, thinly sliced (such as Corrleggey)
salt and freshly ground black pepper

Method Heat two tablespoons of the olive oil in a large pan and tip in the onions, then cook for 10 minutes until softened but not coloured, stirring occasionally. Stir in figs and garlic until well combined and then pour in the red wine and balsamic vinegar. Simmer for about 10 minutes or until most of the liquid has evaporated. Stir in the sugar and half of the thyme. Season to taste and leave to cool completely.

Preheat oven to 200C/400F/Gas 6. Arrange the French bread slices on large baking sheets in a single layer. Drizzle over them the remaining oil and bake for 6-8 minutes until the bread is pale golden and crisp. Leave to cool slightly.

Spread the sweet onion mixture over the bruschetta and arrange the goat's cheese on top. Season with pepper and scatter over the remaining thyme. Place on large baking sheets and bake for another 4-5 minutes or until the goat's cheese has melted.

To Serve Arrange the sweet onion and goat's cheese bruschetta on a large platter.

Tip Even if time is on your side, don't be tempted to make these too far in advance, as the toasted bread goes soggy.

Baked Salmon with Herbs and Citrus Fruit

Serves 8-10

This baked salmon not only looks and tastes fantastic but it is also deceptively easy to make. Use it as your main centrepiece for a summer buffet and serve with a selection of salads, such as Chunky Potato Salad (page 91), Feta Cheese, Red Onion and Avocado Salad (page 93) and Pasta Salad with Baby Spinach (page 95).

Ingredients
2 tablespoons olive oil
2oz / 50g couscous
finely grated rind and juice of 1 lemon
finely grated rind and juice of 1 lime
1 red onion, finely chopped
1 garlic clove, finely chopped
1 tablespoon chopped rinsed capers

2 tablespoons chopped fresh parsley
1 tablespoon chopped fresh tarragon
1 egg, beaten
4lb / 1.75kg salmon, cleaned, filleted and skinned
salt and freshly ground black pepper
sliced cherry tomatoes, fresh dill sprigs, wafer-thin cucumber slices and lime wedges, to garnish

Method Preheat oven to 180C/350F/Gas 4. Cover a large baking sheet with foil and drizzle with one tablespoon of the olive oil.

Place the couscous in a heatproof bowl and pour over 9fl oz / 250ml of boiling water and set aside for 5 minutes to soak, then fluff up the grains with a fork. Add the lemon and lime rind and juice, red onion, garlic, capers, parsley, tarragon and egg. Season to taste and stir well to combine.

Place one salmon fillet skinned-side down on to the oiled foil-covered baking sheet. Spread over the couscous mixture in an even layer and lay the remaining salmon fillet skinned-side up on top of stuffing. Carefully bring edges of foil together over the salmon, making sure that the foil does not touch the top of the fish and scrunch the edges together to seal. Bake on the baking sheet for 45 minutes until the parcel is puffed up and the salmon is cooked through and tender. Remove from the oven and leave to cool in the foil.

To Serve Open up the foil parcel and carefully transfer the baked salmon to a large serving platter. Garnish with the sliced cherry tomatoes, fresh dill sprigs, wafer-thin cucumber slices and lime wedges.

⬤ Tip This dish can be prepared the day before and kept covered with clingfilm in the fridge until your guests arrive. However, leave arranging the garnishes until you are just ready to serve, for the maximum effect.

Chunky Potato Salad

Serves 8-10

This is my standard potato salad recipe, which once mastered can be adapted for different results. Try adding a bunch of finely chopped spring onions or three finely diced hard-boiled eggs and a tablespoon of chopped fresh parsley.

Ingredients
1lb / 450g baby new potatoes, halved if large
1lb / 450g sweet potatoes, peeled and cut into chunks
(orange fleshed, if possible)
5 ripe tomatoes, cut into wedges

½ pint / 300ml mayonnaise (shop-bought or home-made)
2 tablespoons Dijon mustard
1 tablespoon chopped fresh dill
salt and freshly ground black pepper

Method Cook the new and sweet potatoes in a large pan of boiling salted water for 10 minutes or until just tender. Drain and rinse briefly under cold running water. Leave to cool. Place in a large bowl with tomatoes and season to taste.

Place the mayonnaise in a bowl with the mustard and dill. Mix well to combine and then stir in two tablespoons of water to thin down the dressing slightly. Pour over the potato mixture and gently fold in using a large metal spoon, until well combined.

To Serve Transfer the chunky potato salad to a large serving bowl.

Tip There are two main types of sweet potatoes. Both are suitable for this recipe, although the orange-fleshed variety has a more dramatic colour and mildly sweeter flavour than the pale yellow type.

Feta Cheese, Red Onion and Avocado Salad

Serves 8-10

This summer salad conjures up images of tavernas in the warm sun, where it is always drizzled just with olive oil. Don't be tempted to dress it before serving as it will just begin to wilt before your eyes.

Ingredients
2 ripe avocados
1 tablespoon fresh lemon juice
4 Little Gem lettuces
1 red onion, thinly sliced
2oz / 50g pitted black olives
8oz / 225g feta cheese

For the French Dressing
8 tablespoons extra virgin olive oil
3 tablespoons red wine vinegar
1 garlic clove, crushed
½ teaspoon Dijon mustard
pinch sugar
salt and freshly ground black pepper

Method To make the French dressing, place the olive oil, vinegar, garlic, mustard and sugar in a screw topped jar or bottle. Season to taste and shake well to combine.

Cut the avocados in half and remove the stone, then using a dessertspoon carefully scoop out the flesh. Cut into slices and place in a large bowl with the lemon juice, stirring to coat.

To Serve Break up the Little Gem lettuces into individual leaves, discarding the outer leaves, and place in a large serving bowl. Scatter over the avocado slices, red onion and olives, then crumble the feta cheese on top. Pour the French dressing into a serving jug or bottle and place at the side so that people can help themselves.

Tip The secret to a good salad is to use as little dressing as possible – the leaves should barely glisten.

Pasta Salad with Baby Spinach

Serves 8-10

This pasta salad is good served warm or cold and appeals to children and adults alike. Add some chopped griddled chicken if you would like to make it more substantial.

Ingredients
1¹/₄lb / 550g pasta bows (farfalle)
6 tablespoons olive oil
2oz / 50g pine nuts
2oz / 50g raisins
2 bunches spring onions, trimmed and
finely chopped

2 garlic cloves, crushed
8oz / 225g baby spinach leaves
good pinch freshly grated nutmeg
3oz / 75g freshly grated Parmesan
salt and freshly ground black pepper

Method Plunge the pasta into a large pan of boiling salted water, stir once and cook for 10-12 minutes until *al dente*. Drain and rinse briefly under cold running water. Drain again and place in a large bowl.

Heat half the olive oil in a frying pan and fry pine nuts for 2-3 minutes until lightly golden, shaking the pan occasionally. Add to the pasta with the raisins. Add the remaining olive oil to the frying pan and sauté the spring onions, garlic and spinach for 2-3 minutes or until the leaves have just wilted. Season to taste and quickly drain off any excess moisture, then fold into the pasta mixture. Add the nutmeg and Parmesan and then mix gently to combine. Season to taste.

To Serve Transfer the pasta salad to a large serving bowl and use as required or cover with clingfilm and chill until needed.

●Tip I just love this simple salad with its variety of textures and flavours. The spinach can be left raw and the garlic omitted if you prefer, but I like to wilt it long enough to bring up its colour.

Thyme-Spiced Roast Rib Eye of Beef

Serves 8-10

This is perfect for serving large groups so that you can relax and enjoy the company with no last-minute hurdles. I also like to serve this with my Garlic and Smoked Bacon Potato Gratin (page 99) and a lightly dressed rocket salad.

Ingredients
5lb / 2.25kg boned and rolled rib eye of beef
3/4 pint / 450ml red wine
1/4 pint / 150ml red wine vinegar
1 tablespoon sugar
2 bay leaves
1 tablespoons chopped fresh thyme
2 tablespoons cracked black peppercorns
1 teaspoon ground allspice

For the Horseradish Cream
7fl oz / 200ml crème fraîche
4 tablespoons horseradish sauce
1 tablespoon snipped fresh chives
salt and freshly ground black pepper
roasted root vegetables, to serve

Method Place the beef in a large non-metallic dish. Pour the wine into a jug and add the vinegar, sugar, bay leaves and half of the thyme. Mix well to combine and pour over the beef, turning to coat the joint evenly. Cover loosely with clingfilm and leave to marinate in the fridge for at least 4 hours and up to 48 hours is best to allow the flavours to develop, turning occasionally.

Preheat oven to 190C/375/Gas 5. Remove the beef from marinade, and wipe off any excess with kitchen paper. Mix together the rest of the thyme with the cracked black peppercorns and ground allspice on a flat plate. Use to coat the beef as evenly as possible, then place in a roasting tin. Roast for 2½ hours for medium rare, basting occasionally; or give it an extra 30 minutes if you prefer your meat well done.

Meanwhile, make the horseradish cream. Place the crème fraîche in a bowl and stir in the horseradish sauce and chives. Season to taste and spoon into a serving dish, then cover with clingfilm and chill.

To Serve When the beef is cooked, transfer to a warmed serving platter and cover with tinfoil, then leave it to rest in a warm place for about 30 minutes. Carve into slices and arrange on warmed serving plates. Add some of the roasted root vegetables and hand around the bowl of horseradish cream at the table.

Tip The quality of the beef is essential for this dish. It is well worth a trip to the butcher to put in an order of exactly what you want.

Garlic and Smoked Bacon Potato Gratin

Serves 8-10

This has to be one of my favourite accompaniments at the restaurant, where I often serve it with beef or lamb. One of its great advantages is that it can be made in advance and reheated in individual portions on a baking sheet. It also keeps well in a cool oven.

Ingredients
1 pint / 600ml milk
1 pint / 600ml cream
4 garlic cloves, crushed
good pinch freshly grated nutmeg
8 rindless smoked streaky bacon rashers

2lb / 900g potatoes, cut into wafer-thin slices
butter, for greasing
4oz / 100g Cheddar, grated
salt and freshly ground black pepper

Method Preheat the oven to 160C/325F/Gas 3. Pour the milk and cream into a pan and add the garlic and nutmeg. Season to taste and just heat through but do not allow the mixture to boil, then quickly remove from the heat.

Meanwhile, preheat the grill. Arrange the bacon rashers on a grill rack. Cook for about 5 minutes until crisp and lightly golden, turning once. Drain on kitchen paper and when cool enough to handle cut into pieces.

Arrange a third of the potatoes in a buttered large ovenproof dish, season and scatter over half of the bacon, then add another third of the potatoes in an even layer, season and scatter over the remaining bacon. Arrange the rest of the potatoes on top in an attractive overlapping layer and pour over the hot milk mixture.

Cover the potato gratin with a piece of foil and bake for 1 hour until cooked through and lightly golden, then sprinkle with the Cheddar and return to the oven for another 10 minutes or until the Cheddar is bubbling and golden brown.

To Serve Divide the potato gratin into portions and use as required.

Tip Thinly slice the potatoes using a mandolin cutter, being very careful of your fingers or use the slicing attachment of your food processor, as doing them by hand with a sharp knife can be a very laborious task indeed.

Exotic Fruit Pavlova

Serves 8-10

A good pavlova should have a crisp shell with a pinky hue to it and a gooey, toffee-ish centre. This is achieved by adding a touch of cornflour and vinegar to the meringue. Use any fruit selection you like to decorate, but I think that a tropical selection works particularly well with the sweetness of the pavlova.

Ingredients
2 passion fruit
2 kiwi fruit
1 orange
1 star fruit
1/4 pint / 150ml cream
1 vanilla pod, split in half
and seeds scraped out

1oz / 25g caster sugar
finely grated rind of 1 orange
7fl oz / 200ml crème fraîche
8 large strawberries
4oz / 100g raspberries

For the Meringue
4 large egg whites, at room temperature

pinch salt
8oz / 225g caster sugar
2 teaspoons cornflour
1 teaspoon white wine vinegar
4 drops vanilla extract
fresh mint sprigs and grated white chocolate, to decorate

Method Preheat the oven to 150C/300F/Gas 2. Line a baking sheet with non-stick baking parchment and draw a 9in / 22cm circle. To make the meringue, whisk the egg whites and salt in a large clean bowl until stiff peaks have formed. Whisk in the sugar, a third at a time, whisking well after each addition until stiff and very shiny. Sprinkle in the cornflour, vinegar and vanilla extract and gently fold in with a metal spoon.

Pile the meringue on to the paper within the circle, making sure there is a substantial hollow in the centre. Place in the oven and immediately reduce heat to 120C/250F/Gas 1/2 and continue to cook for 1 1/2-2 hours until crisp but a little soft in the centre. Turn off the oven, leave the door slightly ajar and leave to cool completely.

To make the filling, halve the passion fruit and scoop out the pulp into a small bowl. Peel and slice the kiwi fruit, segment the orange and cut the star fruit into slices. Place the cream in a bowl with the scraped out vanilla seeds, sugar and orange rind and whip until thickened, then fold in the crème fraîche.

To Serve Peel the paper off the pavlova and transfer to a serving plate. Pile on the cream mixture and arrange all of the prepared fruit and berries on top, finishing with the passion fruit pulp. Decorate with the mint sprigs and grated white chocolate, then cut into slices and arrange on serving plates.

Tip The meringue can be prepared the day before and kept in a cool place until needed.

Iced Chocolate Terrine

Serves 8-10

There is something about chocolate that is addictive. It contains several stimulants, including caffeine and pleasure-inducing endorphins! This wonderful chocolate terrine really couldn't be simpler to make and once it is tucked away in the freezer you don't have any last-minute worries.

Ingredients
9oz / 250g ready-to-eat dried prunes
8fl oz / 225ml freshly brewed tea
2fl oz / 50ml dark rum
7oz / 200g plain chocolate (at least 70% cocoa solids)
2oz / 50g butter
1oz / 25g golden caster sugar
2 eggs, separated

3 tablespoons cocoa powder
8fl oz / 225ml cream
grapeseed oil, for greasing
whipped cream and fresh mint sprigs,
to decorate
raspberry coulis, to serve

Method   Place the prunes in a non-metallic bowl and pour over them the tea and rum. Stir to combine, and cover with clingfilm, then set aside for at least 1 hour or overnight is best. Drain thoroughly and roughly chop. Set aside until needed.

Break 5oz / 150g of the chocolate into pieces and melt with half of the butter in a heatproof bowl set over a pan of simmering water. Leave to cool slightly. Finely chop the remaining 2oz / 50g of chocolate and set aside.

Place the rest of the butter in a bowl with the sugar and using an electric mixer beat until light and fluffy, then gradually beat in the egg yolks and cocoa powder. Fold in the cooled melted chocolate mixture with the chopped prunes and finely chopped chocolate.

Place the cream in a bowl and whisk until it forms soft peaks. Whisk the egg whites in a separate bowl until they have formed soft peaks. Fold the cream into the chocolate mixture and finally fold in the egg whites until just combined.

Line a 2lb / 900g loaf tin with oiled clingfilm and carefully pour in the chocolate mixture. Cover with clingfilm and freeze for at least 4 hours or preferably overnight until solid.

To Serve   Decorate the terrine with the whipped cream and fresh mint sprigs, then cut into slices and arrange on serving plates with the raspberry coulis.

 Tip   There are now a number of good quality shop-bought raspberry coulis on the market but if you'd like to make your own simply place a punnet of raspberries with a squeeze of lemon juice and enough icing sugar to sweeten in a food processor or liquidiser and blend to a puree. Then pass through a sieve and use as required.

Crêpes Suzette

Serves 4

This is one of those desserts that never seem to fade in popularity – a classic 1970s number, still going strong.

Ingredients
4oz / 100g plain flour
1 tablespoon golden caster sugar
pinch salt
2 eggs, beaten
1 tablespoon sunflower oil, plus extra for greasing
½ pint / 300ml semi-skimmed milk

For the Sauce
4oz / 100g butter
4oz / 100g golden caster sugar
½ pint / 300ml freshly squeezed orange juice
2 teaspoons finely grated orange rind
1 teaspoon finely grated lemon rind
1 vanilla pod, split and seeds scraped out
3 tablespoons Grand Marnier or Cointreau

vanilla ice cream, to serve
orange-rind shreds, to decorate

Method   Place the flour in a large bowl with the caster sugar and salt. Make a well in the centre and add the beaten eggs, oil and two tablespoons of the milk. Whisk until smooth with a balloon whisk, then gradually beat in the milk, drawing in the flour from the sides to make a smooth batter. Cover with clingfilm and leave to stand for 20 minutes, if time allows.

Heat the minimum of oil in a 7in / 18cm heavy-based crêpe or frying pan. Pour in just enough batter to thinly coat the base of the pan. Cook over a moderately high heat for about 1 minute until golden brown. Turn or toss and cook on the second side for 30 seconds – 1 minute until golden.

Slide the crêpe on to a plate and keep warm. Repeat with the remaining batter, adding a little more oil if necessary and stacking the crêpes on top of each other with squares of greaseproof paper in between to prevent sticking – you should have eight in total.

To make the sauce, heat the butter and sugar in a sauté pan over a low heat, stirring occasionally until the sugar begins to dissolve. Increase the heat and continue to cook for 4-6 minutes until the mixture caramelises and turns golden brown. Carefully pour in the orange juice, then add the grated orange and lemon rind and vanilla seeds, then allow the sauce to bubble down for 3-4 minutes until slightly thickened, stirring.

Pour the Grand Marnier or Cointreau into the pan and simmer for another minute, then reduce heat to low. Fold the crêpes into triangle shapes by folding each one in half, then in half again. Arrange them in the frying pan and spoon over the sauce to coat evenly.

To Serve   Arrange two crêpes on each warmed serving plate with some of the sauce. Add a scoop of the ice cream and decorate with the mint sprigs and orange-rind shreds.

● Tip To make orange-rind shreds, pare the rind from an orange and carefully shave away any white pith, then cut into thin strips and blanch in a small pan of boiling water for 1 minute. Drain quickly and pat dry with kitchen paper before using.

Baked Lemon and Vanilla Cheesecake

Serves 6-8

The beauty of this dessert is that it is smooth, silky and rich. It's ideal for a dinner party as you can make it the day before and keep it in the fridge until needed.

Ingredients
3oz / 75g sultanas
3 tablespoons dark rum
1lb / 450g full fat cream cheese
9oz / 250g soured cream or quark
5oz / 150g golden caster sugar
4 eggs, separated
1oz / 25g plain flour

1 vanilla pod, split and seeds scraped out
finely grated rind and juice of 2 lemons

For the Base
3oz / 175g butter, plus extra for greasing
8oz / 225g digestive biscuits, crushed
icing sugar, to dust
whipped cream to serve

Method   Place the sultanas in a small bowl with the rum and set aside to soak for at least 4 hours or overnight is best.

Preheat the oven to 160C/325F/Gas 3. To make the base, lightly butter a 9in / 22cm spring-form cake tin. Melt the butter in a pan over a gentle heat. Add the crushed digestive biscuits and mix well. Spread the mixture evenly over the base of the tin, pressing down with the back of a spoon to flatten.

To make the filling, place the cream cheese in a bowl with the soured cream or quark, caster sugar, egg yolks, plain flour, vanilla seeds, lemon rind and juice. Beat together with an electric beater until smooth and well combined.

In a separate bowl, whisk the egg whites until you have achieved stiff peaks. Using a large metal spoon, carefully fold the whites into the cream cheese mixture until just combined. Finally fold in the soaked sultana mixture.

Spoon the filling on top of the biscuit base, using a spatula to spread it out evenly. Bake for 1 hour - 1 hour 10 minutes until golden brown and just set. It should be slightly wobbly in the middle. Turn off the oven and leave the cheesecake to cool completely in the turned-off oven.

To Serve   Carefully remove the baked cheesecake from the tin and transfer to a serving plate, then cut into slices and arrange on serving plates with a dollop of cream and dust with icing sugar.

Tip Be careful not to overcook this baked cheesecake as the filling will become dry – make sure that it still has a slight wobble in the middle before switching off the oven.

White Chocolate Tiramisu

Serves 6

To bring this dessert up to date I like to serve it in Martini glasses, but you could always just layer it up in one single glass dish if you prefer.

Ingredients
1/4 pint / 150ml cream
6oz / 175g white chocolate, grated
11/4lb / 500g mascarpone cheese
12 sponge fingers

For the Custard
5 egg yolks
1 tablespoon cornflour

3 tablespoons caster sugar
1/2 vanilla pod, split and seeds scraped out
1/2 pint / 300ml milk
31/2 fl oz / 100ml cream

For the Poached Raspberries
1/2 pint / 300ml red wine
3oz / 75g caster sugar

1 cinnamon stick
1/2 vanilla pod, split and seeds scraped out
10oz / 300g raspberries, plus extra to decorate
cocoa powder and fresh mint sprigs, to decorate

Method To make the custard, place the egg yolks in a large bowl with the cornflour, sugar and vanilla seeds. Whisk with an electric mixer for 5 minutes until pale and thickened. Place the milk and cream in a pan and bring to the boil, then remove from the heat. Gradually whisk into the egg yolk mixture until smooth, then pour back into the pan and place over a gentle heat. Cook gently until the custard coats the back of a wooden spoon, stirring. Transfer to a large bowl and leave to cool.

To poach the raspberries, place the red wine in a pan with the sugar, cinnamon and vanilla seeds and bring to the boil. Reduce the heat and simmer for 15 minutes until slightly reduced and thickened. Place the raspberries in a heatproof bowl and pour over the wine mixture. Stir to combine and leave to cool.

Place two tablespoons of the cream in a small pan with half of the white chocolate and stir over a low heat until smooth. Remove from the heat and whisk into the custard. Leave to cool.

Whisk the remaining cream in a bowl until it forms soft peaks. When custard is cold, whisk in the mascarpone cheese, remaining grated white chocolate and the whipped cream until smooth. Spoon the poached raspberries into the bottom of individual Martini glasses, then arrange sponge fingers on top, breaking them up as necessary. Spoon over enough of the white chocolate mixture to cover and chill for 1 hour until set.

To Serve Dust the white chocolate tiramisus liberally with cocoa powder and then decorate with the raspberries and the mint sprigs.

● Tip Mascarpone is a rich, creamy cheese originating from Lodi in the Lombardy region of Italy. It has a sweetened taste and is famously used in tiramisu.

Sticky Toffee Pudding

Serves 6

I normally make individual puddings but you can also make one big one. This quantity will fill a 10 x 7in / 25 x 18cm buttered non-stick baking tin that is at least 1in / 2.5cm deep. Bake for 35-40 minutes or until well risen and firm to the touch.

Ingredients
5oz / 150g butter, plus extra for greasing
6oz / 175g dates, stoned and chopped
(preferably Medjool)
1 teaspoon bicarbonate of soda
6oz / 175g light muscovado sugar
6oz / 175g self-raising flour
2 eggs, beaten
1 teaspoon vanilla extract

For the Caramel Sauce
10oz / 300g golden caster sugar
9fl oz / 250ml cream
3oz / 75g unsalted butter
½ vanilla pod, split with seeds scraped out
vanilla ice cream or whipped cream, to serve
fresh mint sprigs, to decorate

Method Preheat oven to 180C/350F/Gas 4 and lightly butter 6 x ¼ pint / 150ml dariole moulds. Place the dates in a pan with ½ pint / 300ml water and bring to the boil, then simmer for 5 minutes until softened. Remove from the heat and stir in the bicarbonate of soda until the mixture stops foaming. Leave to cool a little, then tip into a food processor or liquidiser and blend for 2 minutes to a thick puree.

Place the butter and muscovado sugar in a bowl and cream together for a few minutes until light and fluffy, using an electric mixer. Add one tablespoon of flour and then slowly add the beaten egg, beating well to combine. Fold in the remaining flour with a metal spoon and finally fold in the date puree with the vanilla extract.

Divide the pudding mixture among the prepared dariole moulds and arrange on a baking sheet. Place in the oven and bake for 25-30 minutes until well risen and firm to the touch. When the puddings are cooked, remove from the oven and, after 5 minutes, turn out on to a wire rack to cool completely.

To make the caramel sauce, place the caster sugar in a pan with ½ pint / 300ml water. Bring to the boil, then reduce the heat and simmer for about 15 minutes until golden brown. Stir in the cream, butter and vanilla seeds until well combined, then continue to cook gently for another 2-3 minutes until shiny and thickened, stirring occasionally.

To Serve Arrange the puddings on warmed serving plates. Pour over some of the caramel sauce, then flash under a grill until bubbling, if liked. Add a scoop of ice cream or a dollop of whipped cream and decorate with the mint sprigs. Serve the remainder of the caramel sauce separately in a jug, hot or cold.

Tip If you are worried about the puddings sticking to the dariole moulds, try lining the bottom of each one with a circle of non-stick baking parchment. This will guarantee perfect results every time.

Fruity Bread and Butter Pudding

Serves 4-6

An English classic, that should have a soft set texture with an exquisitely light spicing of nutmeg and vanilla, a few finely chopped prunes and sultanas and a wonderful buttery top.

Ingredients

3oz / 75g butter, softened, plus extra for greasing
4 eggs
1/2 pint / 300ml milk
1/4 pint / 150ml cream
finely grated rind and juice of 1 lemon
1 vanilla pod, split and seeds scraped out

6 tablespoons clear honey
9oz / 250g sliced white bread
3oz / 75g ready-to-eat dried prunes, finely chopped
3oz / 75g sultanas
1/4 teaspoon freshly grated nutmeg
4 tablespoons apricot jam
pouring cream or vanilla ice cream, to serve

Method Preheat the oven to 180C/350F/Gas 4 and lightly butter an ovenproof dish. Beat the eggs, milk and cream together in a large jug. Mix together the lemon rind and juice, vanilla pod seeds and honey in a small bowl and then add to the egg mixture, beating lightly to combine.

Spread the slices of bread with the softened butter and cut off the crusts, then cut into triangles. Scatter half of the prunes and sultanas into the bottom of the buttered dish and arrange a layer of the bread triangles on top. Pour over half of the egg mixture, pressing it down gently, then repeat the layers with the remaining ingredients and sprinkle the nutmeg on top.

Place the dish into a roasting tin and fill with warm water so that it comes three-quarters of the way up the dish. Bake for 35-40 minutes until just set. Heat the apricot jam in a small pan and then brush the top of the pudding with a pastry brush.

To Serve Cut the bread and butter pudding into slices and arrange on warmed serving plates with pouring cream or ice cream.

Tip This is also fabulous made with day-old croissants or brioche.

Chocolate Coffee Roulade

Serves 6-8

This delightful rich chocolate coffee roulade always goes down a treat, and even if you are watching the calories a little goes a long way...

Ingredients
butter, for greasing
4 eggs, separated
4oz / 100g golden caster sugar
5oz / 150g walnuts, finely chopped
1oz / 25g cocoa powder
4 tablespoons fresh white breadcrumbs

2 tablespoons freshly brewed strong black coffee
1 teaspoon vanilla extract

For the Filling
½ pint / 300ml whipping cream
1 tablespoon dark rum or Tia Maria

1½ vanilla pods, split and seeds scraped out
3oz / 75g chocolate truffles, finely chopped
icing sugar, raspberries and fresh mint sprigs, to decorate

Method Preheat oven to 180C/ 350F Gas 4. Lightly butter and line a Swiss-roll tin with non-stick baking parchment. Place the egg yolks in a large bowl with the sugar and whisk together until very pale. Mix the walnuts in a separate bowl with the cocoa powder and breadcrumbs, then fold into the egg yolk mixture. Stir in the coffee and vanilla extract.

Whisk the egg whites in a clean bowl until you have achieved stiff peaks, then fold into the egg yolk mixture. Pour into the prepared tin and bake for 20-25 minutes or until well risen and firm to the touch. Leave to cool in the tin for 5 minutes. Sprinkle icing sugar over a sheet of non-stick baking parchment and turn the roulade out on to it. Cover with a clean damp tea towel and leave to cool completely.

To make the filling, place the cream in a bowl and stir in the rum or Tia Maria and vanilla seeds. Gently whisk with an electric mixer until stiff, then spread over the cold roulade. Scatter the truffle pieces and press them gently into the cream mixture. Using the paper to help, roll up the roulade to enclose the filling.

To Serve Transfer the roulade on to a serving pate and dust with icing sugar, then cut into slices and arrange on serving plates. Decorate with raspberries and mint sprigs.

Tip As an alternative filling I like to use equal quantities of mascarpone and whipped cream mixed with 2 drained canned pitted black cherries.

Ricotta and Summer-Berry Tart

Serves 6

These tarts can be eaten warm or cold and, of course, you could use any soft fruit that is in season, or a good store-cupboard standby would be a drained can of apricot slices in natural juice.

Ingredients
9oz / 250g ricotta
1 teaspoon cornflour
2 eggs
4oz / 100g golden caster sugar
1 vanilla pod, split and seeds scraped out
finely grated rind and juice of 1 lemon
finely grated rind of 1 orange
1 tablespoon dark rum
4½oz / 125g raspberries
4½oz / 125g blueberries

For the Pastry
3oz / 75g butter, diced and chilled
6oz / 175g plain flour, plus extra for dusting
pinch salt
½ teaspoon ground cinnamon
2oz / 50g caster sugar
1 egg yolk
2 teaspoons whipped cream
whipped cream, to serve

Method   To make the pastry, place the butter in a food processor or liquidiser with the flour, salt, cinnamon and sugar and pulse until just blended. Add the egg yolk and cream and blend again briefly. Be careful not to over work or the pastry will become tough. Gather up into a ball and wrap in clingfilm, then chill for 1 hour to rest.

To make the filling, place the ricotta in a clean food processor or liquidiser with the cornflour, eggs, caster sugar, vanilla seeds, lemon rind and juice, orange rind and rum. Blend until smooth.

Preheat the oven to 190C/375F/Gas 5. Roll out the chilled pastry on a lightly floured surface and use to line 6 x 4in / 10cm individual quiche tins. Chill for another 10 minutes to allow the pastry to rest, then line each one with a circle of non-stick baking parchment that is first crumpled up to make it easier to handle. Fill with baking beans or dried pulses and arrange on baking sheets. Bake for 10-12 minutes until the pastry cases look 'set' and are lightly coloured.

Raise the oven temperature to 180C/350F/Gas 4. Carefully remove the paper and beans from the pastry cases and pour in the ricotta mixture, sprinkle with the raspberries and blueberries and bake for another 15 minutes or until filling is just set around edges but still wobbly in the middle. Leave to cool at room temperature.

To Serve   Carefully remove the tarts from the tins and arrange on serving plates with dollops of whipped cream.

Tip Even if you think that making pastry is very difficult and doomed to failure it's worth giving this pastry recipe a go. As it is made in a food processor, the handling is kept to a minimum, so it's almost impossible to go wrong.

Other books in the Neven Series from Poolbeg

Following on from his success as the popular chef on RTE's *Open House*, *Neven Cooks* brings together for the first time a selection of Neven Maguire's best-loved recipes. Whether you are cooking for yourself, for dinner parties or for fussy children, this book has you covered.

With this cookbook **Neven Maguire's** success becomes clear – delicious food, simply explained, beautifully illustrated.

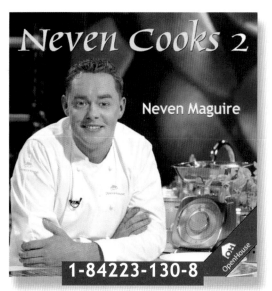

A second collection of stunning recipes from award-winning chef **Neven Maguire.**

Using readily available ingredients and written in Neven's trademark straightforward style, *Neven Cooks 2* includes some old favourites as well as exciting new ideas. Much loved by fans of his bestselling book *Neven Cooks*, this new collection illustrates why **Neven Maguire's** name is a byword for elegant, classy cooking, without any fuss.